A Private Glossary

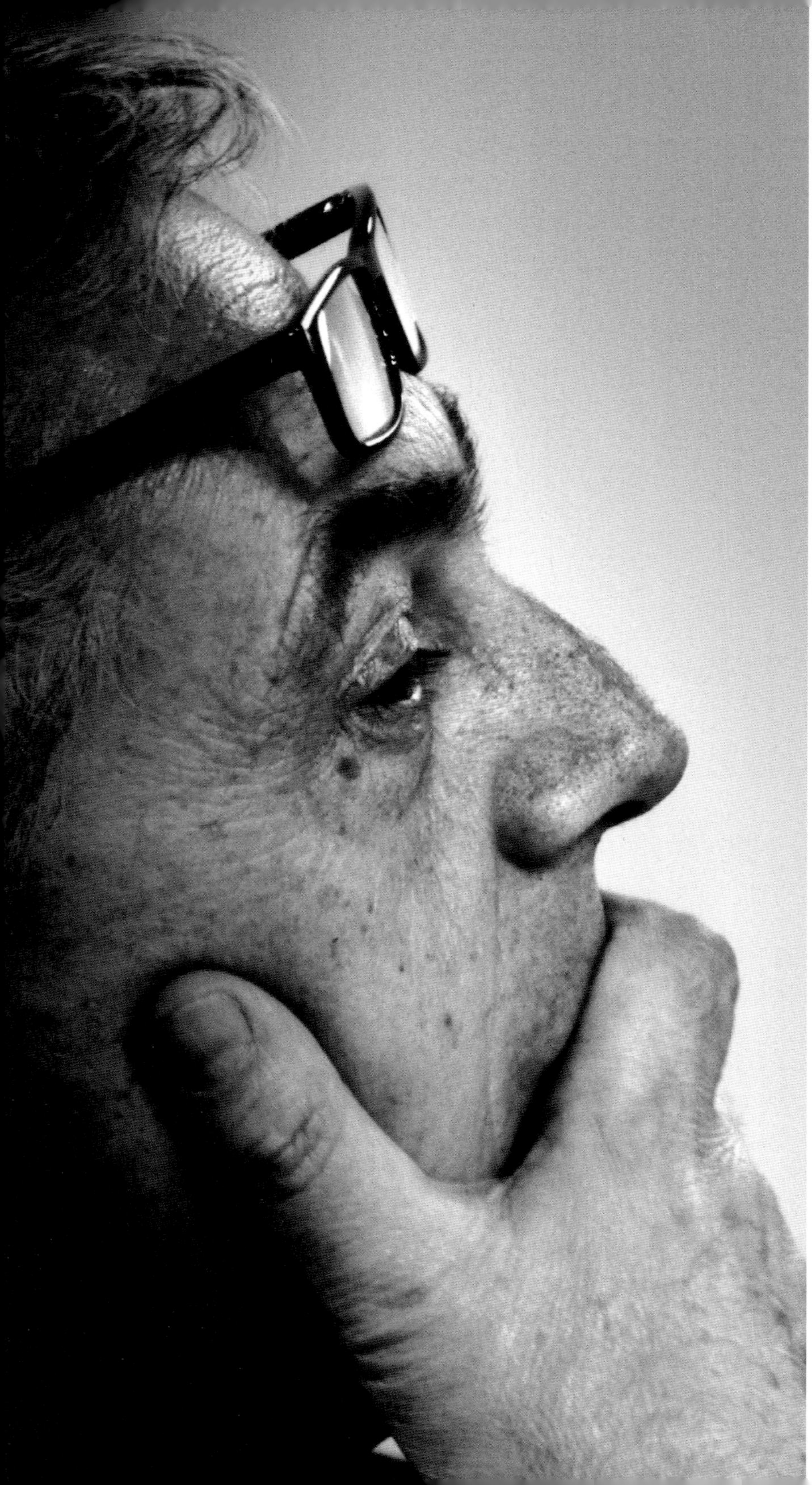

STEFANO

BOERI / GITAI

AMOS

A Private Glossary

Rizzoli

Dialogues

Glossary

Dialogues

Stefano Boeri // Amos Gitai

Building Futures

June 2017

SB *The Book of Amos* left me in awe of the potency of its imagery. I am truly captivated by your ability to harness the faces and visual expressions of individuals as integral components of a historical tragedy.

I'd like to discuss your capacity to use the bodies and faces of people as—we might say—a direct expression of collective tragedies.

It's not a fresco, not a video, not simply text with images or part of a documentary. It's like a kind of *dynamic fresco*.

AG This is a twelve-minute single-shot film, no cuts. I think we need to reinterpret archaic texts, you know? The whole thing started with a phone call from Los Angeles. Guillermo Arriaga, who wrote the film *21 Grams* directed by Iñárritu, said he was working on a collective project about God and wanted me to be part of it. I told him, "Guillermo, I'm not very religious." He called again the next day, and I said, "Listen, I will pay homage to the original Amos." Guillermo asked, "Who owns the rights to the text?" I replied, "You'll have to look for a shepherd who lived in Hebron 3,000 years ago . . ."

So, the film is the result of this project. Like in architecture, art, or cinema, when people give you a pretext to do good work, you just go for it. I have long been interested in reflecting on the beauty of these ancient texts. In the film, there are seven actors and actresses who portray the fearless character of Amos, the biblical prophet who denounces social injustice. Some speak in Hebrew, others in Arabic, using only the biblical text. This film, *The Book of Amos*, is a portrait of the entire Middle East, which was not so different 3,000 years ago. It is a work of reinterpretation.

SB Since you mentioned Iñárritu, I'd like to challenge you with a description of an art piece he created in 2017 for the Prada Foundation in Milan, which I'm not sure you're familiar with. Iñárritu's work immerses visitors in a virtual, augmented reality—or something in-between—allowing them to experience, for about ten minutes, the journey of a Mexican family attempting to cross the border into the United States.
You enter a room and you encounter various technical devices that replicate reality, enabling you to choose your perspective as you observe this group of people navigating the desert. Eventually they are caught by the police, who arrive in helicopters. It's a profoundly affecting experience, steeped in pain and suffering. Yet, despite being emotionally engaged, I found myself skeptical of the ability of augmented reality and virtual reality to truly immerse you in the scene.
Reflecting on your work in art and cinema, I can't help but feel that these attempts to bridge the gap between the viewer and reality fall short compared to what you achieve through your art. So, my question is, what is your stance on these kinds of experimental approaches?

AG I didn't know this piece. Iñárritu is a friend, but for me, the missing element is the political dimension. I believe that the divorce of art, of all arts, from the political context is what contributes to phenomena such as Brexit, Trump, and so forth. People feel that artists have these interesting lives—which is true—but are completely disassociated from real life. There are more and more codes that they cannot interpret, leading to the rise of demagogues like Le Pen, Erdoğan, or Netanyahu. I believe the arts need to engage with reality. By "engage" I don't mean indoctrinate. For instance, I'm against Michael Moore's approach to documentary because I find his films manipulative. Going back to *The Book of Amos*, I really like that ending because it deals with understatement after a long sequence with a very high, dramatic tone.

SB It's blurry, blurring into reality.

AG It's also about recontextualizing. Stefano, for as long as I have known you, as an architect you have always been interested in politics; isn't that important? Otherwise, this field is left to trivial, uneducated politicians who understand nothing about the arts. They think that artists live on a planet of their own, but it's necessary to challenge this view.

SB I wanted to ask you something about your film on the Rabin assassination. The term "docufiction" attempts to capture this blurring condition between documentaries and pure narrative fiction, although you have always escaped from this kind of definition, in a way. *Rabin, the Last Day* stands as a masterpiece in this regard. How do you perceive yourself within these different categories, and what do you think the future holds for you?

AG I'm just an architect, so . . .

SB *[Laughs]* I know.

AG For every project, I must decide what is the best medium to do it—whether it should be a documentary, fiction, or a different form. Sometimes, as with *Rabin, the Last Day*, I conduct extensive research, but ultimately, I have to decide how to transpose it into a mise en scène with actors. There is no formula.

Cinema, like architecture, is a collaborative medium. You need to assemble a team with a shared focus and direction, people who have different talents—some very visual, some narrative. It's all about the relation or the "tension" between narrative and form.

That's why I have little to no interest in projects that are purely formal or solely thematic. The tension between form and narrative is what I find most challenging.

SB Indeed, this analogy can be extended to architecture. We understand the pivotal role of being an editor-in-chief, orchestrating the collaboration of talented individuals and fostering a cohesive team dynamic. However, despite this collaborative effort, there are moments when the weight of decision-making falls squarely on your shoulders.

AG In a way you almost have to like being alone.

SB *[Laughs]*

AG You need this characteristic. Some decisions are analytical, but a lot of them are intuitive. When a film is finished, people start making assumptions about what you did. But these meanings are not always intentional. The films I create are designed to invite interpretation because I don't like films that treat the viewer as a passive consumer.

There are times when I will be sitting on a plane watching a film, and I enjoy it in the moment, but the next day I can't even remember what it was. The films I appreciate most—whether my own or others'—begin after the screening ends. Why? Because then you have to figure out what this person actually wanted to tell you, you have to reconstruct it, like in *Rabin, the Last Day*. What is the meaning? What are the different layers?

As an artist or a filmmaker, you need to construct the form and then destroy it. Otherwise, it becomes too aestheticized. There are a lot of parameters and equations.

SB Well said. Thank you very much.

The Resurgence of Fireflies

May 2020

SB Caro Amos, if it weren't for this deadly virus lingering in the air worldwide, we'd be together in Venice these days for the Architecture Biennale.

The last time—during Okwui Enwezor's Art Biennale—we were with Alexander Kluge, and after enjoying a spritz and a plate of *sarde in saor* in a *calle*, we crossed the water to Giudecca to greet Rem Koolhaas. We spent the night drinking and chatting in a *bàcaro* . . . Today it is scary to think that we've lost, at least for the time being, that way of being together. Will it return? Are you planning to attend the film festival? What are your thoughts on the future of cinema without the communal, dark chamber that is the movie theater, and the collective unconscious it provides?

AG Ahh, Venice, Venice . . . in spite of the virus . . . we don't want to follow Thomas Mann regarding Venice and death.

But I think, dear Stefano, that Venetians, at some point, have had enough of being looked at as zombies in a living but old museum. Now that Venice is back to reality, the city can try to *carpe diem*, meaning to make the most of this crisis and reinvent itself and its relevance.

It's a fantastic place that always makes us celebrate limitations: no cars; mostly boats; the smell of salt and sea water; lagoons. All of these things remind us that perhaps the most exciting thing about this city is that it obliges you to think differently about moving. And, after all, this crisis invites us to find new ways of moving in space.

You asked me about cinema, and my answer will be about cinema and architecture: *carpe diem*—let's try to rethink it by connecting to its civic meanings in both of our mediums. I look forward to seeing you this autumn in Venice, exploring new ideas of architecture and presenting a film.
Regarding presentation, cinema, unlike theater or music or opera concerts, is not necessarily a live experience. It's about "the work of art in the age of mechanical reproduction," to quote Walter Benjamin. I'm sure that it will manage to reinvent itself and find new ways of viewing . . . but let's leave some mystery to our joint architectural project.

SB Yes, for now, it's best to leave the mystery untouched . . . But I must share something with you: during these days of lockdown and forced confinement, I've been revisiting the fourteen extraordinary seminars Roland Barthes delivered at the Collège de France in 1977 on *Comment vivre ensemble* (How to Live Together, a title that, long before the pandemic, is said to have inspired the theme of the upcoming Architecture Biennale).
In those lectures, Barthes gathers fragments of narratives and descriptions of spaces concerning the impossible balance between life in solitude and life in community. Reading certain passages, I was reminded of two "sequence plan" fragments from your filmmaking: the desperate, lonely weeping of Natalie Portman gazing out a cab window headed for Jordan in *Free Zone*, and the choral scene of protesters and police flowing in front of the camera in *The Book of Amos*.
Thinking about those images, I wondered how in the future we can ensure both the "right distance" of bodies and the "necessary intensity" of affects and emotions. I believe and fear it will be a balance that requires complete reinvention.

AG I agree with you that Barthes's title is very suitable for being put before architects in Venice, and I'm sure that they will pro-

vide insightful answers to the question of "how can we live together." When I visited you at the Triennale, after my own sessions at the Collège de France, we discussed about space and structure, cinema and architecture. Even in the Israeli context, the urban lessons about the organization of space in the kibbutz—how we can design a whole community with almost strictly pedestrian access—are still relevant.
As you suggest, I think that revisiting ideas from the past—in this specific case, Barthes—might offer valuable proposals for the future.

I want to return briefly to your earlier question.
We can think together of a way to create a new kind of camera obscura, one that allows us to *carpe diem*, to capture *hasard* or the accidental in our cinematic experience.
The sequence you refer to in my film *Free Zone* with Nathalie Portman illustrates this: a woman is sitting in a car and through the expression on her face we can complete and project many narratives and emotions. But this sequence is also the result of a fusion of different circumstances (melancholic weather, her particular state of mind, hand-held gentle camera, etc.). This is the case in many of my films—the one on the assassination of Rabin, *Kadosh*, *Kippur*, and even my latest films, *Why War* or *Shikun* . . .
The question I pose to you, Stefano, is how we might achieve a similar process in architecture, a medium that is becoming more and more premeditated, more and more subservient to design extravaganza. How can we keep the spontaneity of *carpe diem*, of seizing the moment?
How can art, architecture, cinema regain that healing aura? How can we reclaim meanings that have been slipping through our fingers in this post-capitalist age and its exclusive urge for greed?
Let's go back, in a bit of an obsessive manner, to the original meaning of *carpe diem*. Horace's full phrase, "*Carpe diem, quam minimum credula postero,*" is often translated as "Seize

the day, put very little trust in tomorrow." The ode says that the future is unforeseen and that we should not leave future happenings to chance, but rather do everything we can today to make our future better. This phrase is usually understood in relation to Horace's Epicurean background.
However, if we relate this to the age of Coronavirus, perhaps the first written expression of the concept is Siduri's advice to Gilgamesh, telling him to forgo his mourning and embrace life, "reversing the liminal rituals of mourning and returning to the normal and normative behaviors of Mesopotamian society." In a Talmudic manner, let me ask you, dear Stefano: Do we really want to go back, or shall we rather seize the moment and its painful lessons and move forward, looking for new ways of existing on this planet?

SB You know, Amos, I believe this pandemic presents us with profound questions about the shaping of time and history.
Firstly, one might argue that this event is a monumental challenge to what you and I have gleaned from studying Fernand Braudel and the other historians of the Annales school—namely, that history isn't forged by isolated events but by the enduring processes of structures over time. However, upon reflection, it is also true that this pandemic is closely related to two other global crises affecting the life of the human species: the financial crisis of 2008, and the consequent collapse of confidence in the relationship between quantitative growth and development, and the climate crisis, which has become increasingly dire since 2015, marked by events like COP 21 in Paris and Pope Francis's *Laudato Si'*. The pandemic crisis, therefore, doesn't refute the Annales perspective; rather, it underscores that a single event, born from a lengthy chain of events, can spill over from the ordinary and catalyze a catastrophic shift in history.
Secondly, there's the question of perceiving the present and the future, as you've touched upon.

For me, *carpe diem* means being aware of the "instantaneous" nature of the future we experience. In other words, it is as if suddenly the very long time of the planet's history and the cyclical, present time of human daily life have short-circuited. The future feels compressed into the present moment. We're living in an "instantaneous" future, a future constructed by the simultaneous and present gestures of billions of humans. Indeed, the diet we choose, the way we move around the land, our relationship with nature determine the trajectory of planetary warming, glacier melt, ocean levels, and the survival, or demise, of our species. And all this depends on us, here and now. Perhaps only the very young have fully realized this.

AG This makes me think of what Ivan Illich talks about in his book *Medical Nemesis*.

Let's try to say it differently,
What one could not put into
The human minds
In sufficient density and urgency
Regarding the consequences of the destruction
of the environment
Was now made by a tiny virus
Much smaller than a millimeter
Or perhaps even much less
That managed to put on their knees
Substantial global interests
Politicians who see themselves
As sophisticated Machiavellian manipulators,
Gigantic interests
Of multinational companies
And an elaborate banking system
All these are crawling
And begging

To restore the same old system,
The resurrection of the old order.

We are left
To wait and observe,
Asking ourselves
If this tiny virus
Invisible to our eyes can create change of such
mammoth colossal powers.
What can a new thought of architecture, urbanization,
culture, cinema contribute to this reflection . . .

Let's go back to the process and methods of design or filmmaking. Both are not intimate arts; both involve many people. In film you have writers, set designers, people behind the camera, actors, editors, etc. Similarly, architects work with structural engineers, sewage specialists, constructors, etc.
Both mediums start with a written text—the architect has a program, the filmmaker a screenplay. The question they both face is how to translate this narrative into form. How to *give shape* to a *story*.
Both depend on the economic limitations of the project, and in some cases, they are subjected to political intervention or censorship. In conflict areas like the Middle East, such issues recur frequently, and you have to collect every grain of resistance. Often, interventions try to meddle with the form, the rhythm of the film, and its associative nonlinear structure as a modern form of storytelling—à la Joyce or Proust—juxtaposing fragments. All of this demands a strong backbone. But I'm convinced that it is worth it; otherwise, we'd just be recycling clichés. Architects face similar dilemmas.
In the times we're living in, these dilemmas are heightened. As resources become scarcer and scarcer, there's no time to waste, and we urgently need new, radically fresh attitudes. Will the tiny

virus manage to challenge all these assumptions and make us more responsive to the only planet on which we find ourselves together? A question for you and for Barthes . . .

SB I think it's up to us. This virus, while cruel, should serve as a stark reminder of our role as the dominant species on this planet. It's reminiscent of Andrei Tarkovsky's work, particularly *Solaris*, which delves into the intimate connection between humans and nature. We've grown accustomed to treating nature as something separate, to be conquered or fixed—I recall our last International Exhibition, *Broken Nature*, at Triennale Milano, curated by Paola Antonelli—when in fact, we are an integral part of it.

Or perhaps Michel Foucault's insights are relevant here, especially his exploration of madness as an expression of human nature—a nature that manifests itself as an unexpected emergence of an uncontrollable energy, subversive of social codes, rising from within our bodies and minds. The truth is, the fate of our forests, oceans, and cities lies in our hands.

Instead of lazily returning to the "normalcy" that has at its core many of the causes of this disaster, we should have the courage to take an evolutionary, Darwinian leap.

Think about it: after a universal tragedy, the human species changes course—it stops consuming fossil fuels, deforesting the planet, wresting land from other living species, waging war for a God that threatens to witness the extinction of its own worshippers. We set out to rebuild cities as kaleidoscopes of biodiversity, reinhabit mountain hamlets by restoring living spaces to wild plants and animals, explore oceans and space not to colonize them but to bring us closer to the very meaning of existence.

It's an immense challenge, yet it's within our grasp today. As you've rightly said, we are a species capable of shaping dreams. If we connect the most progressive ideas born from recent crises, we already possess the visionary and incremental policies necessary for regeneration, including economic revitalization, on a global scale.

AG It's great that you reminded us of the exceptional *Broken Nature* exhibition that you held at the Triennale last year. It was a profound experience—almost prophetic—that highlighted the urgency of confronting the destructive activities of our beloved humankind. What I found even more audacious was your decision to place the exhibition in a venue that typically serves to promote the very architecture it critiques. Also, the assembly of documents, artistic works, cinematic and sound experiences was deeply stimulating.

So now the question remains: What can be done?

You mentioned Jerusalem, this incredible site that has inspired humanity for three millennia. It's remarkable how it has managed to indoctrinate almost two-thirds of the planet with strong monotheistic religions. I come back to this place time and time again: first with the documentary trilogy *House*, which I began forty years ago, followed by *A House in Jerusalem* and *News from Home News from House*, then with *Berlin-Jerusalem*, the film I did with Pina Bausch, and recently with *A Tramway in Jerusalem*.

But since you do a great job of talking about cinema, let me offer some thoughts on architecture.

When I completed my diploma in architecture in the mid-seventies, I was offered a position as a senior architect for the City of Jerusalem. My chief asked me to prepare a program for the rehabilitation of a neighborhood called "Beit Israel," which borders the ultra-Orthodox area of Mea Shearim.

I thought the best way to approach this would be to inject funds into the neighborhood, employing the large number of craftsmen and builders that were actually residing in this place. This would provide necessary maintenance for the infrastructure and economically support the residents. However, I was later summoned by the head of the department, who informed me that my task was different: I was to indicate which parts of the neighborhood should be destroyed to facilitate the construction of a new mall. I resigned. A few years later, while studying for a Ph.D. in Architecture at Berkeley, I came across Ivan Illich's *Tools for Conviviality* and E. F. Schumacher's *Small Is Beautiful*. These texts offer a theoretical background for what can be done after the plague, so we don't forget to *carpe diem*. Let's seize the moment.

Much like the great housing initiatives from nearly a century ago, such as the Weissenhof quarter in Stuttgart, which brought together Le Corbusier, Mies van der Rohe, Walter Gropius, and others with the simple challenge of "how to create livable environments with spaces no larger than 70 square meters." The same was repeated in several other places, like the Viennese Karl Marx Hof Housing project, which still serves as a major living area.
So, dear Stefano, I embrace your proposition. Let's plan a strategy together when we meet in Venice.

P.S. This can be our homage to Pasolini, who asked us not to forget the fireflies that inspired him in his childhood days. If we do our job well, the fireflies will re-emerge, just as gazelles are now re-emerging on the hills of Jerusalem.

SB Yes, I believe—as you do—that good architecture must arise from a cinematic and anticipated vision of the life that will take place in it; from "fitting" a particular sequence of behaviors and emotions within a landscape. And now, I believe, is the time to explore new sequences. Time to collectively envision behaviors that were, until recently, unforeseeable. Let's meet in Venice soon!

The Memory of a House

April 2023

SB Dear Amos, it's been two years since our last exchange. In the midst of this pandemic and the ensuing isolation, it's important to reflect on the growth of our children and to envision the landscapes of our imagination: the coast, the valley, the forest, the future of the city.

The Covid-19 experience was dramatic for me and, as often happens with dramatic experiences, extremely instructive. In the autumn of 2020, I lost my mother, and the pandemic took many of my dearest people.

In November, it also led me to tackle one of the most beautiful and challenging tasks of my life as an architect. During the darkest period of Covid-19, in December 2020, the Italian Prime Minister, Giuseppe Conte, asked me to design the image and spaces for the first vaccination campaign. It involved designing a modular and repeatable architecture to serve as a vaccination pavilion, as well as proposing a visual that would become the symbol of the rebirth of an entire nation through the vaccine.

Thinking about Italy's situation at that time and the challenge we were invited to tackle, I immediately thought of the title of a famous text by Pasolini, *Un paese di temporali e primule* (A Country of Storms and Primroses), and decided to work on the powerful yet delicate image of a primrose, the first flower to bloom after a long winter.

We worked like madmen for weeks to create both the graphic design and the architecture of the pavilion, closely collaborating with the National Medical Scientific Committee overseeing the vaccination campaign. In early January, we presented the project

live. It was the first project in the world to address the issue of suitable vaccination sites and the need to communicate the urgency of vaccination in the most effective and direct way possible. I remember it was immediately published in The New York Times. The Primroses project was both a success and a failure; a success because the stylized image of the flower accompanied the entire vaccination campaign; a failure because it soon became clear that it would be much more economical (as we had ourselves suggested) to install the vaccination structures within existing, unused spaces rather than building hundreds of new pavilions.
In February 2021, a few days before getting my vaccination, I fell seriously ill with Covid-19, along with a dear friend who was also a brilliant and famous photographer, Giovanni Gastel. We were both hospitalized, but Giovanni, with whom I exchanged daily messages to try and lighten the situation, didn't make it. I survived and was reborn through a long and difficult convalescence. In five months, I lived five years.

AG These days I am in Venice to set up *House*, an installation for the Architecture Biennale that will open in a few days. The installation is based on a documentary trilogy I filmed in 1980, 1997, and 2005, spanning 25 years, that captures the life of a house in Jerusalem through its successive owners. It then became a play that we staged last month at the Théâtre national de la Colline in Paris.

SB What significance does this location hold for you?

AG The political contexts that surround us now are even more mephitic. Perhaps this is one of the reasons we are reminded of the story of *House* . . . As far back as forty years ago, in its various formats and media, the *House* project aimed to encourage a dialogue between Israelis and Palestinians. It has been transposed into a theater work with Israeli and Palestinian actors, an Iranian musician, and a choir.

In a constructive and subversive way, we are trying once again to seize the moment and propose a creative project—a *House* that viewers must interpret, not simply consume.

SB The house you return to and that we see in your film is a small construction, but it is one so powerful that it resists hatred, attacks, and prejudices. The house is a device for relationships between different people, which, despite changing the characteristics of those who live there, never ceases to convey a sense of community to them. It stands as a rare beacon amidst the vast literary landscape of diabolical houses, which, instead of protecting and uniting those who live there, hide and sometimes fuel misdeeds, secrets, and deep resentments under their roofs. Beyond its myriad metaphors—a mirror of our souls, a realm of dreams, a projection of our identities—the house fundamentally serves as the crucible for family creation: whether small or large, simple or embracing every gender, faith, or culture. And I can't help but think that deep down, we are both children of architects who built houses for their family.

AG I like your observation. What I realized while working on this trilogy is that the only way to heal the tragic rift between Israelis and Palestinians is what Palestinian poet Mahmoud Darwish proposed in his poem "Think of Others."
And I would add: think about how they perceive their home, their personal memories. This must be the starting point of a healing process we so desperately need, and it shouldn't be one-sided.
It is true that we are both children of architects who built houses to give us shelter. I still remember the non-religious and very moving ceremony for your mother in Milan, when people talked about her years as a partisan, and how she passed on her architecture and social beliefs to her children. We, too, like most human beings, are children of stubborn mothers.
In one of her last letters, my mother wrote to me:

"To answer your question—change country?—sometimes I think about it, but where to go? This is where my closest friends, my architect husband, and many others are buried. I don't go to cemeteries. No! Dry, hollow bones . . . But this is where the memories are fixed, and it is difficult to tear them away. Only a few trips abroad, there and back.
For me there is probably no other place, but restlessness devours me: what will happen to you, to young people, the flesh of our flesh, who have remained and are living the disappointed dream? Will you be able to defeat the darkness that envelops us?"

SB Yes, I remember your mother's beautiful words well. Back in the 1960s, my own mother, Cini, designed a small, beautiful concrete house in Sardinia for our family that resembles a bunker—but instead of protecting us from the outside, it became the epicenter of my parents' divorce. Nevertheless, it has endured as a space that encapsulates the memories of a family that continues to expand over time—because while human families grow and evolve, houses remain immutable mineral shells. I believe these structures should retain their stability, even if they're eventually passed on to other families. I find it profoundly sad to witness houses partitioned and divided among distant relatives after just a few decades. Putting walls where glances once crossed, where meetings took place, is simply terrible. It's a sort of anti-architecture of family—a disintegration of the very essence of familial connection.

AG To answer you, my dear Stefano, I want to pay a small tribute to Munio, my architect father, who never wanted to design his house or own anything. Munio was against the recovery of Palestinian houses by the Israeli left-wing *Nomenklatura*. He rebelled against the destruction of the Arab market in Haifa and decided to remain faithful to a minimalist architecture in hom-

age to his masters and friends of the Bauhaus, designing dining rooms for the kibbutzim.
So I grew up in a more nomadic, but still rich, context of meaning.

SB Your father was not only a civil hero but also a leading figure in the best European rationalist architecture. His architectural legacy in Israel stands as a testament to the extraordinary European modernism infused with Arab, Middle Eastern, and Islamic nuances. I am reminded, for example, of the wrought iron embroidery of the parapets or gates that we still find in the central districts of Cairo, Tehran, Beirut. Sadly, these vestiges of history, influenced by Western ideals, are gradually being effaced by the passage of time and the autocratic regimes in power. This confirms the paradox that architecture—an art destined to last over time—sometimes demonstrates great fragility towards politics, which is instead the sphere of immediate actions.

AG You're right. And look, the only house Munio designed for the family was in Kiryat Bialik, near Haifa, for his mother. She wanted a large German iron oven for cooking. It was spectacular to see how she prepared the fire in her house. That was perhaps one of the first performances he witnessed as a child. Now the question remains: How do we channel memories and impressions into the creative process? And how can we create a proposal for a utopian vision with these fragments of memory traces and visions in which the house becomes a metaphor and a microcosm?
Let's go to Venice together for the inauguration of the Biennale, and I will show you my temporary *House* . . .

Architecture and Cinema

February 2024

SB I believe religions play a significant role in global events, and I state this precisely with regard to the concept of community.

Reflecting on the ideas of American sociologist Robert David Putnam, who emphasized the importance of community, it's clear that community thrives on two parallel energies related to the notion of social capital: *bonding* and *bridging*. The first concept, "bonding social capital," refers to a force that strengthens the historical, cultural, and religious identity of a community. Bonding capital ties a community to its own identity, rooted in history, place, family, and social groups—essential for a community's soul.

The other force focuses on bridging—bridging social capital—which involves establishing connections with other communities. While the first force explores investing in our roots, the second one considers using the perspectives of others to reflect on ourselves. It emphasizes empathy.

Putnam's concept of social capital indicates that capital isn't merely a financial notion but also encompasses cultural heritage, relationships, and community. The crucial point is the balance between the two forms of social capital—bonding and bridging—preserving one's own identity without avoiding the urgency to engage with the identity of others.

Religions encompass both these spheres, yet recent trends suggest a weakening of the bridging aspect. They have often contributed to creating barriers rather than fostering connections. In the geopolitical context, it's evident that the current situation extends beyond Israel and Gaza, having roots that trace back to September 11. Gaza is merely one episode in this broader tragedy, which highlights how religions, as systems of thought, are often inherently resistant to empathy. Or at least that's my take. I am an atheist, so I have no particular connection to religion.

Anyway, some months ago, we were invited to Lumbini, a small city in Nepal, to design an important center for Buddhism at the site where the last relics of Buddha were preserved for thousands of years.

It is a very peculiar and fascinating location on a hill: a simple hill with a tree covering the relics.

We went there to present an idea for a master plan. We had envisioned the place becoming something like Mecca, with thousands of monks coming there twice a year.

Our master plan for the Ramagrama Stupa in Lumbini is very simple but, I believe, symbolically powerful. We kept the sacred tree and the hill at the core of a large mandala-shaped plain surrounded by a ring of trees and plants with high biodiversity.

It's interesting to see how, on the one hand, Buddhism, which is both a philosophy and a religion, has historically worked on bridging, creating connections, and trying to take the point of view of others, including other living species. But on the other hand, if we observe Buddhism today, we can also recognize a field of conflicts, as there are many different schools and traditions that sometimes clash with one another—see, for instance, how the Dalai Lama is not recognized by the Chinese Buddhist community.

Anyway, they all came to the Ramagrama Stupa in Nepal where, in front of the sacred tree and facing an amazing huge plain, we were presenting the project. Every Buddhist community had its own platform, its own "island." That was a visual representation of how, even within a religion that aspires to promote the necessity of dialogue between different perspectives, gaps still exist. But ultimately, they were all there, embraced by the same space, sharing the same hope and the same project.

AG The cinematographic project of the *House* (*Bayit*) trilogy began precisely at the point you are making, namely: How can we look at the same space, the same architectural object, a house, which evokes different memories and narratives?

I filmed the first part of this documentary trilogy in 1979–80, almost forty-five years ago, followed in 1998 by *A House in Jerusalem*, and the third episode, *News from Home, News from House*, in 2005, twenty-five years after the first film. This last part is dedicated to the fading memory of the original house and the growing Palestinian diaspora in Amman.

The house at the center of this story was located in Dor Dor Ve'dorshav ("Each Generation and Its Interpreters Street") in West Jerusalem. It was originally owned by a Palestinian gynecologist, Dr. Mahmoud Dajani. After the 1948 war, during which Dr. Dajani and his family fled the house following the Deir Yassin massacre, the Israeli government settled the Toboul family there, who had immigrated from Colomb-Béchar, Algeria. By the time I was filming the first part of the trilogy, an Israeli economist, Professor Haim Barkai, had bought the house and decided to convert it into a villa. But in order to execute the reconstruction works, he brought Palestinian workers from the refugee camps around Hebron and stones from the mountains of Yatta in the West Bank. Serge Daney really captured the essence of the film when he first saw it in 1980, writing: "Gitai wants this house to be both a symbol and something very concrete; he wants it to become a character in a film. He achieves one of the most beautiful things a camera can register 'live,' as it were; people who look at the same thing but see different things—and who are moved by that vision. In this crumbling shell of a house, real hallucinations begin to take shape."[1]

So, in a way, this house is both a microcosm and a metaphor for human and political relationships. The concept of "lieu de mémoire," as elaborated by French historian and intellectual Pierre Nora, is perhaps one of the best ways to describe the toxic conflict between Israel and Palestine.
Later on, I found that transposing this theme into other disciplines could be a relevant challenge. Around the same time, Wajdi Mouawad, the Lebanese-Canadian author and theater director, invited me to conceive a theatrical performance while Leslie Lokko asked me to create an installation for the Venice Architecture Biennale in 2023. I found it fascinating to navigate from one medium to another, studying the different forms of creation and communication through film, theater, and exhibition, all dealing with the same single house in Jerusalem.

SB Let's go back to our family stories, which I think are a central part of our heritage. There's something profound about our connection with our parents. It's something peculiar and unique, incomparable, but at the same time, we share the same roots, in a certain way. Both our parents played significant roles in geopolitics and in Europe during a very delicate period of European history (the 1920s, '30s, '40s, and World War II) and just after.
They were part of a European professional bourgeoisie trying to reinvent the world; they truly believed in and trusted the future. I believe our generation serves as a bridge between their era of regeneration in the '50s, '60s, and '70s, and the evolving perspectives of our children, who approach the future with distinct outlooks.
My parents met during World War II; they were both partisans. After the end of the war, they married in a small church in the mountains of Lago Maggiore, where some months earlier they had been fighting against the Nazis. Their story and the circum-

1 *Libération*, March 1, 1982.

stances of their encounter were always very present for me. This memory and awareness are probably stronger than what I learned from them in terms of knowledge or professional skills—one was a neurologist and the other an architect.
Their life trajectory was extremely influential on my personal evolution. I am sure it was the same for you. I have read what you have written about your mother; she was a strong person. The legacy of our parents, yours and mine, implicitly transmitted by their life trajectory, is crucial.

AG Yes, absolutely. Efratia was born to Jewish labor pioneers who came from Russia in 1905, after the pogroms that followed the failure of the first Russian revolution. They understood that Europe was becoming a dangerous place for Jews. They took a boat from Odessa to Alexandria, and family mythology says they traveled by camels to Jaffa.
Efratia was born in the same year that Tel Aviv was created, in 1909. She had me when she was in her forties, and she probably passed on to me this energy of not being fearful, of allowing myself to speak out about a kind of Israel that was the center of her identity—a modern, open, and secular country. In her mind, Israel was created as a nonreligious or even anti-religious political project, in line with her vision as a socialist anarchist feminist utopia.
Munio Weinraub, my father, grew up in Silesia and studied architecture at the Bauhaus in Dessau. He came to Palestine as a refugee after being beaten by the Nazis, at the time when Goebbels closed the Bauhaus. He brought with him the spirit of his teachers, Mies van der Rohe and Hannes Meyer, a spirit of integrity, a sense of duty for minimalist architecture responding to social needs, and the creation of the kibbutz movement.
My parents spent their honeymoon in Baalbek, Lebanon. I remember one time, at the little kitchen table where we used to

have breakfast, Efratia placed two train tickets where it was simply written "Haifa–Beirut." I asked her, "Mama, this is an enemy country, how come you traveled there? The border is closed." She answered, "It was possible, and one day it will be possible again." She transmitted this openness and a sense of optimism to defy the dark visions.

Efratia,
like others of her generation born in the Land of Israel,
was neither a woman of the Diaspora nor an Israeli.
Israel did not yet exist.
Her generation will invent its own identity,
their own sense of belonging.
Efratia wrote letters all her life,
keeping them from an early age,
as if she wanted to retain traces of
her journey;
as if she sensed that her inner world
may embody the fate of her country.
Efratia's letters attest to the life
of a woman, my mother:
her intimate reflections and doubts,
her thirst for independence,
her heated debates with her father
about the destiny of their country.
Her loves, cult of friendship,
motherhood,
and later periods of mourning and loss, old age,
and troubled times.
I can still hear her voice,
the Ancient Hebrew of a daughter of the first
generation of labor pioneers
who wanted their child to speak a Modern Hebrew
for our time.

That brings me to my recent conversation with Jean-Luc Godard about architecture and cinema. We discussed architectural issues together: How can an architect design an apartment for this fictional figure of a human being who has 1.2 children, 0.2 dogs, a kind of a mathematical average creature who does not really exist? And how can architecture and cinema still adapt to particular individual situations and preserve some of their artisanal creative talent? We can find traces of this effort in the early Rem Koolhaas elastic space, but how can we continue on this path?
Godard told me that he is not seduced by market forces, that he makes his cinema the way he sees it and would not submit to the mega capitalistic structures that want cinema to follow very rigid and uniform dogmas. At some point, Godard took a big puff of his cigar, his head completely surrounded with a white cloud of smoke, and he said to me, "You know, Amos, I am very interested in the Kabbalah." After a moment of hesitation, I told him, "I am not very surprised; sometimes when I see one of your recent works, like *Adieu au langage*, I feel that when you did the editing, you first decided intuitively to put one scene next to another and only after you did it were you searching for the meaning or the signification of your own gesture." We started to laugh. But this leads me to the real question: How can we preserve the creative intuitive procedure in the age of—if I am to quote Walter Benjamin—"mechanical reproduction"?

SB The intertwining of cinema and architecture stands as a cornerstone of our friendship, a dynamic relationship ripe for exploration. To inject a refreshing perspective, I propose a counterpoint: delving into your insights on architecture. While admittedly challenging, such a dialogue promises to transcend the confines of a mere focus on cinema, enriching our discourse with diverse perspectives and intellectual depth.

In the nineties, I organized an event focused on the concept of "site inspections," when you have a script and try to find a location for your movie before starting. I invited Wim Wenders to talk about *Lisbon Story*, together with João Luís Carrilho da Graça, a talented Portuguese architect. I was interested in exploring how the initial contact with a place can partially or radically alter the screenplay of a film or the abstract concept of an architecture.

It's something present in our (yours and mine) preliminary experience of an idea, of an intention. We go to a place and see if our idea works or not; whether we can maybe modify or correct it, or whether we should find another place.

Indeed, when you spoke about your movie—this amazing story of a woman moving from Spain—you went to see the location where you planned to shoot. This connection with a place is preceded by a concept or a narrative. You arrive with something in mind and observe how the place reacts.

This approach is fascinating because you're not constrained by the location; instead, you see how the place reacts to your idea, your intention, your plans, and your projects.

This kind of reciprocity between places and concepts is, for me, something that is common in our two disciplines.

Our common friend Richard Ingersoll worked extensively on the idea of montage in urbanism and architecture. He coined the term "cut and copy urbanism," which explored cinema and architecture in an interesting way. He navigated between cinema (he worked with you on your first film *Esther* and wrote a beautiful book on your father, Munio Gitai Weinraub) while being a close friend of both of us.

AG I met Richard when we were both doing our PhDs at Berkeley. He was always such a stimulating and generous thinker. We met and talked to each other until his very last days. The book he did on my father is such a profound monograph . . . When you read it you understand the life and the struggles of an architect and the destiny of his country.

Stefano, what I like is that we are trying to establish a cross-discipline dialogue through common friends and encounters. That's becoming rare nowadays, because of a general tendency to overspecialize. We are curious people. We want to be stimulated by tangential thoughts. And this is part of our relationship. When you have a larger context to apply to your work, it is only enriching.

The Influence of Others

May 2024

SB Considering our age and the span of our existence, it's incredibly striking how everything around us has changed in recent years. When we entered this crazy world, it was all very simple, in a way. On a geopolitical level, there were just two hemispheres—the East and the West. And I believe we shared a common horizon, in terms of an idea of our future: the future was something that we were capable of envisioning and describing; it was very clear. Although it was determined by our intentions and aspirations, and perhaps our utopias too, the future was there.

At the same time, we were the first generation after World War II in a position where we had to build the new world. From many points of view, I think that in seventy years the world has been completely flipped on its head. It's not simply about complexity, but also about a proliferation of factors and variables.

We now recognize three distinct types of intelligence: alongside what we call human intelligence, we can also compare a natural intelligence—that we attribute to animals and plants—and a new artificial intelligence, which is something completely unexpected. At same time, in terms of gender, there's a concerted effort to combat biological determinism, granting individuals the freedom to chart their own paths regarding gender identity. This, I believe, constitutes another revolution.

And then again, if we simply think about the climate, when we appeared in this world, we thought that the planet was still to be explored, and we had no concerns about the future of the environment. We had no idea about the risks of global warming and climate change. Today we recognize these as existential threats to the survival of our species and the environment. Our perception of the universe has also expanded exponentially since the 1950s.

Reflecting on these shared experiences over seventy years, I find it quite remarkable. Our journey is truly exceptional. That explains two things, in my opinion: the first is our *inquiétude*, which is a very fertile condition—this feeling of never being satisfied about what we do or think, and struggling to describe the world around us. And the second, which I think you and I both share, is the necessity to always go back to some roots—whether they are related to family or places.

I think the balance between the two is a unique way to try to think about the future and what will happen, including when we are no longer here.

AG In a way, our dialogue and friendship make a strong statement against the overemphasis on identity.

It's very *à la mode* these days to only bring people together with similar identities—gender, sex, religion, politics. It's something that leaves me quite skeptical, to be honest because if humanity goes in this direction, it will not progress. This old word, "progress," is a bit *démodé* now, but it came about when people traveled and ideas flowed through communication between different cultures.

In Italy, you grew up in a context that was relatively safe compared to where I was brought up. Sometimes cinema critics label me as part of the "68 generation." Do you know what happened to me in 1968? I was drafted into the army to do my mandatory military service for three years. So, we share different backgrounds but we are friends, even good friends, I'd say. And we can come together and create a profound dialogue. I think this is a statement in itself. Because we are able to cross borders, although there aren't really any borders between you and me.

I want to tell you a story. Some years ago, I was invited to Kolkata, in India, to present a retrospective of my films. I was met at the airport by a police sergeant who escorted me to my hotel. When we arrived there, he said that he had a present for me but it should be given to me in my room. So he came to my room and the present was . . . he stood next to the window and started reciting a poem by Rabindranath Tagore by heart. What poem? Surprisingly, a poem about Africa, not India or the Ganges.
I am not at all persuaded that an Israeli police sergeant, or an Italian or French one, for that matter, would have considered it appropriate to gift me a poem about Africa. The real issue, I think, is how to create a dialogue between cultures. Our book, despite its hybrid form, can be about two people sharing thoughts and ideas, even if we were not born on the exact same spot on this planet.
When I make films, I insist on including Palestinian actors. It's a gesture of dialogue. In my film, *Kadosh*, I chose to give the role of Chief Rabbi to a great Palestinian actor, Yussuf Abu-Warda. When I was asked why, I simply replied that he's a great actor. I didn't even want to say that I did it intentionally. He's a great actor, period. If I followed the logic of those who criticized my decision, Jewish actors could only play the role of Shylock. But a good actor, regardless of their background or nationality, can play any role, including Hamlet.
It's becoming very urgent to talk about crossing borders and extending our hands across them. I remember a few years ago, during the municipal elections in Milan, you were working with Giuliano Pisapia as a candidate—who did not listen to your good advice to allocate the Expo money to the restoration of architecture rather than erecting new elephant-like buildings, only to find them empty, but that's another story. At that time, you asked me to write a letter in support of Pisapia. I wrote the letter, which Claudio Abbado and Nadine Gordiner, among many others, signed, and when I came to Milan, you told me

Pisapia wanted to thank me personally for his election victory that year. I mentioned that I didn't have much time and suggested he meet me at the Cinema Lab's small auditorium in Milan, and he did.

SB Yes, the Anteo Cinema, I remember.

AG Pisapia came with a bunch of journalists, and I remember one of them asking me: "Why are you getting involved in Italian politics? You come from somewhere else, why are you interfering?" I was taken aback and didn't know how to respond initially. Then I said to him, "I always found Stalin's accusation against the Jews interesting. He accused them of being *cosmopolitan*. And I'm very happy to be cosmopolitan. I want something good for my country, but at the same time, I want something good for other countries, too."

I think we have to encourage a cosmopolitan culture where people cross borders and extend their hands to others. For example, the beautiful and crazy project of Esperanto—inventing a universal language to break barriers—is a great proposition. It is urgent to recreate a cosmopolitan Esperanto syntax, which will form the basis of a dialogue about themes and texts that interest many people.

SB Perhaps it's indicative of a shift from a time when national identity was intertwined with notions of the future, ethnicity, faith, and geopolitics, to now, where individuals possess a cosmopolitan, multifaceted identity. It's truly fascinating. And I think that in our ways of intervening in the world—you as a movie director and myself as an architect—we are trying to absorb this multiplicity of perspectives.

Multiplicity is a very important concept. When I started to work as an architect and a researcher, I chose this word to name the research group I founded in the 1990s.

Multiplicity was a group of architects, photographers, geographers, artists, and sociologists who helped me transform my profession from mere problem-solving into a practice that balances openness to the complexity of the world with the need for decisive action. That means deciding the future and defining the configuration of the physical space—whether it's a house or part of a city.

So Multiplicity represented a pivotal moment for me, when I understood that the traditional role of the architect was completely over and we had to redefine the profile of the profession. Yet, in a way, your contribution to cinema may be even more profound. You have intertwined cinema with your personal experiences, connecting with the dramas and hopes of those around you. That's immensely significant.

I believe this explosion of identities has occurred throughout our lifetimes. But what we now share is a commitment to preserving our roots and, at the same time, maintaining our *inquiétude* as a fertile precondition.

AG It's interesting you say that cinema perhaps has a stronger impact than architecture. I don't think you can ever really abandon architecture, but at one point, I did start to do more work in cinema. I suppose I spent nine years studying architecture because of my father, a Bauhaus architect, who died while I was completing my mandatory military service. In hindsight, I realize that I was probably trying to keep speaking to my dead father, to understand what he thought the mission of an architect was. So I enrolled at the Technion in Haifa and completed my diploma—now I was actually an architect, I was allowed to design buildings. While studying at Technion, the Yom Kippur War erupted. I was shot and wounded while I was part of a rescue team in a helicopter that was shot down by a Syrian missile. When I returned from the war, I started making Super8 movies; I wasn't sure if I wanted to become an architect or a filmmaker. Then I received a grant from Berkeley and completed my Ph.D. in Architecture there. Altogether, I studied architecture for nine years, which is a lot. But I don't think I wasted my time; it was very helpful for what I do now. There are some parameters in architecture that you also need as a filmmaker.

SB You're always receiving feedback, from clients and from the public as well.

AG What disturbed me about architecture at the time, coming from all this experience of violence in the Middle East, was the non-immediacy of the medium. You can make an incredible project and then they tell you that it won't be built until some years later—it holds you back. And sometimes, when the project is finally approved, you're already somewhere else. But the architectural discipline or the commissioner do not allow you to redefine the project.

The architect will always face a dilemma: if he starts to modify the project because he has new ideas, he may risk having it cancelled. When I understood this mechanism, which leads to a sort of architectural conformism, I started to become more and more interested in cinema and its ability to create and react with immediacy.

You mentioned the younger generation—poor guys! All disciplines are being threatened by very rigid formats now. Netflix is a kind of capitalistic tyranny where filmmakers have to make movies according to an algorithm. They even recruit neuroscientists for this purpose. I remember once speaking at a conference with a neuroscientist at the Guggenheim in Berlin. He presented an experiment in which he had showed sequences of Alfred Hitchcock's films to people who had electrodes attached to their heads. This allowed him to see which parts of the brain were activated—when people would be emotional or certain feelings were aroused. He was very impressed by his discoveries. I was

rather surprised and even shocked, and I told him that what he was doing was a disaster: production companies would start asking filmmakers to present films to a selected audience and measure their reactions scientifically to enhance marketing.
But if we look at the films of Pasolini, Rossellini, Godard, filmmakers who just didn't give a damn about all this, they gave us fantastic and poetic works.
My journey from architecture to cinema was about finding a way to speak about the contemporary experience more directly. Architects have to be diplomatic and also political, and I felt that in cinema I could say what I wanted without concessions. Maybe people will like it, maybe they won't, but that's it.
Nonetheless, it's unquestionable that during those nine years of academic studies, I learnt a lot. It became like the voyage Konstantinos Kavafis describes in his beautiful poem "Ithaca": "As you set out for Ithaca / Hope your road is a long one / Full of adventures, full of discovery."
At Berkeley, I also studied the Marxist economy of the third world and philosophy of science with Paul Feyerabend. All these things might seem unnecessary, but they are actually very stimulating and valuable. It's good to broaden your knowledge because, at some point in your life, it may help you. I did not become a filmmaker instantaneously.

SB I agree that the similarity between these two professions extends beyond the mere narrative or the shared focus on inhabiting spaces—it is kind of banal. Instead, it lies in the protocols, procedures, client relationships, public expectations, and our roles as organizers and editors of collective intelligence, to which we impart a very definite orientation.
Another parallel arises when we consider the outcomes of our work and the complexities therein—the relationship with the client, the public, and the time we spend to produce an art piece that is not reversible, it cannot be changed. Both cinema and

architecture possess a dual dimension: there's the life of a movie, which is very strong at the time of its release, with reactions from the public and critics; and then the work takes on a second life, characterized by a sort of mythologizing.

For instance, *Kippur* or *Kadosh*, or other movies you have done, now have a life that is completely independent from the real history of their production. They are permanently present in the imaginations of people. Perhaps you're not able to achieve this with all your movies, but for me, *Free Zone* or *The Book of Amos*, for example, will always be there; they are timeless. They become classics in a certain way.

And that happens sometimes in architecture as well: certain architectural endeavors can transcend their physical roots, becoming part of the collective consciousness and existing in a dimension of memory and perception. This, to me, embodies the true notion of success. Success is not about the amount of positive reactions but about the capacity of the works to acquire a new nature, entering a different space, which makes them stay in people's memory—it doesn't matter if they were produced ten, fifteen, or fifty years ago.

On the flip side, this dual dimension also entails repetition. It's almost as if these immaterial giants were always haunting us. We have these clouds above our heads that follow us around all the time, and that's nonsense to me. People would love for me to always repeat the vertical forest format, for instance.

I imagine that *Kippur* or *Kadosh* have become milestones for many, yet they also carry an expectation that can sometimes feel burdensome.

AG This is very true. Beyond the moment when a project or a film is presented to the audience, what is interesting is the way it is gradually absorbed, interpreted, or even imitated. That's always fascinating about the arts.

SB What are you working on now?

AG I am working on a project inspired by the dialogue between Albert Einstein and Sigmund Freud. In 1932, the League of Nations asked Einstein to write a letter to Freud, in which he poses a question. Just one question. Einstein simply asks: "Why do people make war?" I am putting the final touches on my film, *Why War*. The problem right now in the Middle East is that each group is only concerned with its own ethnocentric vision. The Israelis care about the Israelis, and the Palestinians care about the Palestinians. The conflict will never be resolved if each group doesn't also consider the other—which brings us back to what we were saying earlier about the influence of others. If they are only concerned about themselves, anything that happens to the other side is legitimized. This is a tragedy.

SB And that is about identity, of course.

AG About any identity: political, religious, gender. This leads me to the great text by Karl Kraus, *The Last Days of Mankind*. He talks about identity in the apocalyptic age. We live in dramatic times, and no one knows how it will end.

SB Very dramatic indeed. But, as you said, it reflects the inability to put oneself in other people's shoes, to develop the notion of empathy, to change perspective.
I think this is crucial for us as architects, because when we have to design a public space or a part of a city, this balance is very delicate. Also when we design a house. Your work on *House* exemplifies this balance impeccably: the necessity to assert your own identity, your own story, but at the same time, the ability to accept the presence of the other.
You're right in noting that the great novelists of early-twentieth-century European culture, like Musil, Proust, or Mann, had

the capacity to preserve their own identity, but also to accept, thanks to literature, the point of view of the other. This is what constituted Europe. It's at the very foundation of the European project. And it was also born thanks to Jewish culture.

AG The interesting thing about what we may call the concept of "Jewish architecture" is that it is *apatride*—in a way, it's almost anti-architectural. For many centuries, Jewish communities have been deprived of a permanent territory and a homeland, so they have developed a nomadic strategy. They have a distinct nomadic attitude toward form, which is in complete opposition to many cultures that cultivate form instead.

I wrote a couple of pages about the very old Jewish strategy of nomadic temporary settlement. Historically, Jews were harassed and persecuted, so they considered architecture as temporary shelter.

My Ph.D. research dealt with five urban Jewish communities across different historical and geographical contexts. I started with the ancient city of Sanaa in Yemen, where both Jews and Christians were obliged by the Pact of Omar to build their houses one floor lower than their Muslim neighbors.

But the Jews adopted a couple of architectural strategies: they would dig tunnels under the existing buildings to create additional spaces, or, during the feast called *Sukkot*, the tabernacles, when they built light structures on the roofs where they slept for several days to remember their wandering in the desert Sinai. If the neighbors didn't protest, the new space would be solidified over time. It's about small gestures. In terms of shape, their synagogues resembled mosques—they even had a place to wash their feet. The only difference was a little wooden stole to keep the Bible off the floor. But other than that, they blended in perfectly with the rest of beautiful Sanaa, which is now unfortunately completely destroyed.

Next, I studied the Jewish community in Ghardaïa, a city in the Algerian Sahara where Jews, Berbers, and Arabs lived together

without a dominant culture, using similar architecture styles. This city inspired Le Corbusier's design for the church in Ronchamp, France, next to the Swiss border, as evidenced by his drawings. This beautiful, touching, and poetic chapel is completely based on Algerian vertical towers that filter very hot and violent sunlight.
I then went on to examine Venice, where the first ghetto in the world was created in 1516, following a decree from Doge Leonardo Loredan and the Venetian Senate. Jews were not allowed to own land, because they were accused by the Church of contaminating it, and were confined to a segregated area of the city, the ghetto; even the land of the ghetto itself was to be owned by Christians only. Despite all these social and political restrictions, Jewish communities adapted by incorporating Baroque and Rococo styles typical of Venetian architecture into their synagogues. In Jewish tradition, the synagogue is not necessarily a building of power (it can be above a shop or even a gymnasium, there's no architectural restriction).
The fourth community I studied was a *Shtetl* townlet in Poland. Finally, I researched an urban kibbutz near Tel Aviv, established in the 1920s after the great wave of immigration that followed the pogroms in Eastern Europe. This kibbutz was a socialist cooperative where land was owned collectively, and people could cultivate small gardens. Unfortunately, it is now disintegrating due to capitalistic real estate pressures.
In this dissertation, I wanted to show how architecture is really attached to this peculiarity of having a nomadic existence.

SB There is a long history of architecture designed to be temporary or even nomadic, which in reality become more permanent than a mountain. This is precisely the case with the Israeli settlements in the West Bank, which, often initiated as experiments in communal living, have become almost military-like outposts to control the territory.

In 2003, with the Multiplicity research group, as part of a broader study on borders understood as complex devices (thus not reducible to a two-dimensional line dividing two nations), we attempted to decipher the myriad invisible boundaries that make the territories of the West Bank a place of selective discrimination. By following the routes of two taxi drivers, one with an Israeli passport and one with a Palestinian passport, we observed how the population without an Israeli passport, which is unable to access the main roads connecting the settlers' villages (built like real military outposts on the hilltops), had to stop continuously at numerous checkpoints scattered along the lowland road network, taking five times longer to travel the same distance.
I think this is also linked to the concept of community, of common space. This aspect is very important for us. We are used to talking about community, public and social relations, and finally the presence of this very rough, dry, and cold material, which is space. Spaces are not just inert entities; they serve as the canvas upon which social behaviors and relations are painted. And when we talk about identities and the integration of diverse cultures, we inevitably touch upon the significance of physical space. This adds layers of complexity to the dialogue, but as you have demonstrated very well in your movies, space is not passive; it is shaped by social interactions. This dynamic interaction is both complex and sophisticated.
I often quote Winston Churchill's words during the bombing of London in 1943 when, talking about the reconstruction of the city, he said, "We shape our buildings; thereafter they shape us." It's a profound realization, isn't it?

AG Even the Holocaust Memorial, when it was built by Peter Eisenman, was not met with favor among German journalists. They complained because he had chosen the best piece of real estate in the center of Berlin. And I love Eisenman's response: "It's ugly and it will last 1,000 years."

But there's something I also wanted to ask you. The process of designing or making a film is always stimulated by curiosity, by *hasard*, by coincidence. And we also talked about this—*carpe diem*, seizing the moment when you have an idea. Sometimes, in the middle of the night, an idea will come to me, and I feel I have to write it down immediately, otherwise I won't remember it in the morning. Then, when the morning comes, the daylight fleshes out the idea, and I realize that it was actually not a good one. But sometimes it's a very good idea, and I will actually make a project out of it.

So, it's a journey from the subconscious to the conscious—finding, digging in the magma of our imagination. To actually pursue this desire, which I think both of us share, means traveling to unknown territories. It's about human relations. Creativity is about this journey into the unknown and the effort to articulate it. And I think it's probably a similar process in architecture.

When I direct a scene, I always tell my assistants not to comment because I want to observe what the actors will do intuitively. Sometimes they will naturally give a much better performance than if I had premeditated it. I like to integrate *hasard*, which is strongly connected to my curiosity about this journey to the unknown, to speak to people I have never spoken to, to deal with cultures I have never dealt with.

And I can also see it in your work as an architect. I can see that this is something you're interested in.

SB Absolutely. Creativity is an indecipherable process.

For an architect, a new idea might take the form of a three-dimensional image or a sentence that describes a space yet to be realized. It can emerge from the sudden fusion of two distant worlds, cultures, or aesthetics, or it might be the outcome of an arduous effort to reinterpret the ideas and projects of others. More often, however, it arrives unexpectedly, sweeping away hours of deep and serious reflection in an instant.

But returning to the concept of the unknown, it reminds me of the theme of the last Triennale International Exhibition. The title was *Unknown Unknowns*. It was a phrase by Donald Rumsfeld, Secretary of Defense during the Bush administration, who, in the aftermath of September 11, during a US Department of Defense news briefing regarding the lack of evidence linking Iraq to the supply of weapons of mass destruction to terrorist groups, famously said: "As we know, there are known knowns; there are things we know we know. We also know there are known unknowns; that is to say we know there are some things we do not know. But there are also unknown unknowns—the ones we don't know we don't know."

During that time, I engaged in discussions with scientists who explained to me that the notion of absolute knowledge, standing at 100%, is now obsolete. We thought we knew, for instance, 5% of the universe; but now we understand the universe is immensely bigger. We thought we knew 5% of all the synapses in the brain, only to find out that the brain is much more complex. We thought we knew 5% of the depths of the oceans, but we have realized that they extend far beyond what we can fathom. My point is not that we still have to explore the remaining 95%, but that we have lost the notion of 100%. We don't know if what is left to explore is 95% or maybe 395% or 4,095%, in relation to what we know today. We have lost the notion of the limits of knowledge.

What makes me extremely uneasy, and at the same time very open, is the fact that we should probably stop thinking that it is necessary to know everything. This realization is unsettling yet liberating, challenging the Enlightenment-era vision of knowledge acquisition. Now we have to earn, to gain knowledge, and to enlarge our capacity to control and know everything.

But I'm starting to have some doubts about that. Maybe it's not too bad to preserve, respect, and defend the areas where our knowledge remains incomplete. It's an inherent part of life:

there are aspects we don't know and may never know. Maybe it's more natural to be surrounded by mystery or miracles, or *hasard*, as you said. It's not that bad. Also, when I design a building or a part of a city, I find myself intrigued by the aspects I cannot design. It is a little bit like the plastic chair next to the Bible.

AG This is very interesting. It reminds me of a great work by Alvar Aalto: on the main street of Helsinki, he designed the department store for Stockmann. He did something that I greatly appreciate and that is becoming rare nowadays: he respected the height of the two neighboring buildings—which are somewhat neoclassical, so not even that interesting. He went so far as to match the proportions of the windows, using a simple rectangular design similar to those of the neoclassical buildings. It's a sort of timid gesture, but once you step inside, it's completely modern—the furniture, the woodwork, everything.
This raises the question of how to contribute to an ensemble without over-imposing our individual interpretation. For me, it is very touching that Alvar Aalto understood this. On this main street, he could have made something flashy, a bold statement of modernity that everyone would notice. But he didn't. He played by the rules established by previous generations, and I think that's becoming a rarity.
Regarding what you said about knowledge, even when we write a script, we begin with an initial discussion. As you mentioned, and as other intellectuals such as Umberto Eco have noted, we're not in the sixteenth century where intellectuals held the overall knowledge of everything that existed—all the texts, the Bible, the Greeks, everything—because not so much had been published.

SB It was an elite; knowledge was concentrated in the hands of a select few.

AG At that time, they could still have a comprehensive knowledge of most literature that was available. They could act in a very coherent context. To extend Aalto's metaphor: the context was known, and when you know the context, you can contribute in a very precise way. But because we now face this information overload, as you mentioned, along with lots of copies, bad copies, semicopies of ideas that claim to be original, it's exhausting to maintain a commanding knowledge of everything.

So, when we write a new project, there is a discussion about the best strategy: I focus on tackling the details, while Marie-José, my co-screenwriter, wants to understand the entire project from A to Z. She needs to have complete knowledge of the plot, where it will go and how it will end.

SB But at the same time, we need the aspiration to control the whole, which allows us to create trouble and noise.

AG It is helpful to have somebody who brings some structure to our burning, wild brains. Knowing that we don't know everything is important; the worst thing is when people pretend they know everything, which, even theoretically, is impossible at this point.

SB And it is also connected to the trajectory of our generation: we started off with the aspiration to explore and expand our knowledge everywhere, only to realize that most of the universe remains unknown to us.

It's not just about exploration and control; it's about using that knowledge to improve our lives and the lives of others.

Earlier we discussed acceleration, and I believe this concept of uncertainty is a byproduct of the rapid pace of change we've witnessed over the past two decades—from events like September 11, terrorism, the 2008 financial crisis, to the Covid-19 pandemic and ongoing wars, all compounded by the looming specters of climate change and artificial intelligence. Speaking of

which, I'm curious about your thoughts on AI, if it is starting to become important in your world. Personally, I'm very scared. This is really the first time in my life when I see something that I feel is very dangerous.
While I acknowledge its technological advancements and potential benefits, there's an underlying discomfort I can't shake off.

AG It is very invasive. It's a sort of Big Brother—it knows everything we do, what we talk about, what we think.
I spoke with a scientist about the idea of creation for my *Golem* project in Paris. The whole concept of the Golem is the creation of an artificial human being, so, in a way, it is a kind of metaphor for AI.
I asked him, "Can we say that AI can only use elements we know, while our creative process is introducing elements that we don't know already?" His response was that it is not that simple, because some of the elements that we don't know are already based on elements that we do know. So that did not comfort me [*laughs*].
The Golem mythology, which started in the third century, is based on the assumption that people can create something that will escape their control and eventually control them. Can they keep the last word in the creation? That's the real issue.
It's fascinating because I'm integrating many parameters during the research for this project. For example, the beginning of research into uranium led to Marie Curie's discovery of X-rays, which helped medicine, and then it ended with the atomic bomb.
So, we construct something helpful and constructive, and it can end up destroying us.

SB It is a profoundly complex issue, particularly with AI, given its intangible nature. It's not merely a tool; it represents a manifestation of individual intelligence.

Just as an example: thanks to Carlo Ratti, director of the 2025 Architecture Biennale in Venice, I was invited to use ChatGPT for an "impossible" dialogue with Ebenezer Howard, one of my mentors and the inventor of the "garden city" model, who was born in London in 1850. AI had metabolized all of Howard's scripts and projects, along with my own, to the point of being able to engage in a serious, sophisticated discussion with me about the differences between his concept of a garden city and my vision of a vertical forest.

But this Howard avatar was also capable of discussing our passions for music, football, and lifestyles. When I told him I was very sorry to have disturbed someone who passed away 96 years ago, he responded by saying, "Not at all, Stefano, and don't forget that if a parallel world for creative people exists, I'm sure we will meet again there."

I was seriously troubled by this conversation and by the idea that in the near future, AI, together with robotics, will be able to bring back to life and interact with individuals who passed away 2,000, 200, or even two years ago—creating a simulacrum of their souls simply by metabolizing their written or codified thoughts.

AG Irène Jacob, the actress, wanted to gift me a poem for my birthday. She told me to give her a reference of a poem that I liked, and she would use AI to write a new one.

It was truly amazing—I gave her the poem "The Road Not Taken" by Robert Frost, and the poem she sent me back . . . it was beautiful. It synthesized information about me with the parameters given by the original poem. The closing lines of the original poem read, "Two roads diverged in a wood, and I—I took the one less traveled by." The AI poem needed to lean on something we already know in order to sail into an unknown future.

Glossary

Stefano Boeri // Amos Gitai

About Origins

The genesis of a Golem

Amos Gitai

I

Efratia, my mother, like the women of her generation born in the land of Israel, is no longer a woman of the diaspora.
She is also not an Israeli, as Israel does not yet exist. She is a Hebrew woman, which carries an archaic connotation. This generation seeks its own sense of belonging.
Efratia was born in 1909. In the photographs of Haifa from that time, there are very few buildings. There is not a single house on Mount Carmel. The city stretches along the coast, on the Mediterranean.
Efratia's parents left Tsarist Russia and came to Palestine to establish the foundations of a new Jewish society. By embarking on this journey, they broke with two thousand years of existence in the diaspora, according to some. Efratia, like those born in these circumstances, is one of the first children of this modern Jewish immigration wave to Palestine.
There is something unique about this generation in their search for roots or references. Obviously, the Bible, which has been the unifying factor of Jewish existence in the diaspora throughout the generations, is the common text: like a territory of the spirit. This nomadic sense of belonging attached to a text is one of their main references. And since they are secular and socialist, they try to refer only to passages of the Bible that adopt a historical perspective, rather than a religious one. For them, these are texts written by human beings—not by God—over seven centuries, starting from 900 BCE. A deliberate act to record events that mostly take place in the same geographical territory. Therefore, they will use the geographical references contained in these texts as a form of identity.

opposite page
Fabienne Babe, Ophrah Shemesh, Mireille Perrier, and Hanna Schygulla in *Golem, the Spirit of Exile* (1991)

Those of Efratia's generation bear names that are not the traditional names of the diaspora. Instead of Abraham, Isaac, Jacob, Joseph—the traditional names from the Torah—we begin to see names like Avner and Yoav, two generals of King David, or Amos, the prophet known for his fierce criticism of society.
In this context, Efratia, after a stay in Vienna in the late twenties, and despite her keen interest in psychoanalysis, seeks employment. At the age of twenty-three or twenty-four, she becomes a primary school teacher in Haifa, where she teaches literature and the Bible. This gives her the opportunity to apply her secular interpretation—let's not forget that she is a woman while the Bible, in the traditional Jewish school, the *heder*, was taught only by men. She is interested in the question of female identity and produces numerous theater performances with her students, assisted at the time by Munio, my father, an architect and former student of the Bauhaus, for the construction of the sets. I found photos of a set he created for the episode of Bathsheba, when King David, desiring her, sends her husband Uriah to his death in war. Munio made the roofs of Jerusalem on which David first sees Bathsheba. I think he was inspired by the sets designed by Oskar Schlemmer for the performances at the Bauhaus, or by the expressionist images of Feininger.
So Efratia tries, from that time on, to teach the Bible in a non-traditional way, as a historical and ethical experience and reflection. At her funeral, one of her former students recounted that he was seven years old when he immigrated, and the children at school who were born in Israel were a bit tough on him. He remembers that she defended him. He remembers the Bible class where they talked about the Garden of Eden. He asked Efratia, "Why was Adam punished and expelled from the Garden of Eden for a sin he committed before being able to distinguish between good and evil?" And she developed this questioning, which amounts to questioning divine judgment, throughout a semester, during which they reflected on questions of ethics, punishment, rebellion against punishment, etc. It became the material for one of their plays.
She was a fascinating storyteller. The stories she told me left their mark on me and later I began to read certain texts from the Old Testament,

which she considered a literary and philosophical experience. Sometimes, she would tell me these stories instead of reading them to me. I believe I was in kindergarten at the time. I must have been six or seven years old. The Book of Esther and the Book of Ruth are deeply rooted in this period, I think. The kibbutz movement began organizing dance and music festivals in Ein Hashofet. The kibbutzniks read the Book of Ruth in the summer, during the Shavuot holiday, because Ruth meets Boaz in the fields surrounding Bethlehem at the time of the harvest. They tried to preserve certain meanings of this text by linking them to agricultural cycles. They revisited them in a form of popular theater and sat outside to watch the actors move on horseback among the ears of wheat, a kind of rural backdrop. The Book of Esther, which tells the origin of the Purim holiday, was read at the end of autumn, during this holiday.
This experience has inspired all my early films. This sensation of a ceremony during which archaic texts are introduced, the way they fit into the landscape, and the dialectical tension produced by this contemporary reading.

II

For a long time, I have organized my work into trilogies, but they are never completely symmetrical. It's a geometry with an irregular surface, like a triangle.
House (1980), *Wadi* (1981), and *Field Diary* (1982) each deal with a delimited territory within which they observe the internal geometry of the Israeli–Palestinian conflict. But, unlike the first two, the third part of this trilogy, as the title suggests, takes the form of a diary. The perspective is altered: I am no longer looking at a defined site like in *House* and *Wadi*, there is already a sense of movement.
Then follows the triangle of films that encompass territories spanning multiple countries. *Pineapple (Ananas)* (1983) uses the metaphor of the journey taken by a can of pineapples. It's produced in the Philippines, packaged in Honolulu, distributed in San Francisco, and its label is printed in

Simone Benyamini, David Cohen, and Mohammad Bakri in *Esther* (1985), the biblical story set in the ruins of Wadi Salib, in Haifa

Japan. In *Bangkok–Bahrain* (1984), it's human beings who are treated as commodities: Thai women in the sex industry in Bangkok and their men as cheap labor in Bahrain. The third part, *Marlboro*, was supposed to focus on the juxtaposition between a product and the image associated with it. For reasons that are the subject of my film *The Sergeant General Warning* (2001), I couldn't make this final part of the trilogy.

Then comes *Brand New Day* (1987), which observes, through the rock band Eurythmics, how the contemporary music industry selects noises and sounds to recycle and integrate them into a new musical product. The Eurythmics travel to another sound space: Japan. They collect sounds in Buddhist temples, the subway, slot machine noises, and eventually reformat them to create a different sound.

After making this group of documentary films, I left for Europe and gave myself a rule not to make documentaries about Israel as long as I lived there. I wanted to start making fiction. I decided to take a biblical text, the Book of Esther, to start. I was attracted to its beauty, simplicity, and structure. Whatever anyone says, my people have used this text, over the generations, as an expanded territory. Members of Jewish communities scattered around the world, in different geographies and under different regimes, have continued to study and meditate on it while separated or exiled from their original territory. I thought to myself: Why can't I do it? I live in Paris now, why not look at this text which becomes metaphorical if taken from a non-religious point of view and apply it to a form of fiction? I have an intimate knowledge of it, it resonates in my mind, it's a good start.

That's the attraction to this text. But then there's what pushed me away from it. I always need both movements, to love and to not love, to start a project. I don't want to "fictionalize" the experience I observe in my documentaries. For me, fiction is not superior to documentary. I don't want to make *House 2* or *Field Diary 2* as fiction. So I look for an indirect angle to observe reality, an indirect or parabolic structure. And the story of Esther offered this possibility.

Moreover, I like to subvert existing mythologies, to question the validity of certain established truths. In collective memory, the story of Esther is that of the victory of an oppressed people who liberate themselves from their oppressors. But the end of the text is often disregarded: the story of the unnecessary vengeance told by the biblical writer. I wanted to remind people of this part that has been forgotten and question the cycle of vengeance and the permanent permutation of oppressor/oppressed. Not to mention that this story has a very strong cinematic structure. In the film, each scene was composed of a single long take. In a way, some codes of the following films were already present in Esther (1985), such as the question of choreography within the shot and the use of direct sound, irregularities and noises being an integral part of the film material. So the film is a semi-historical episode that has its place in our memories, but without nostalgia, serving as a useful potential for the future.

So why a theological text? Because it's laden with layers. In the text of Esther, there is the original biblical layer and its various versions, including the Christian Greek version, which contains additions: the presence of God is inserted into the story whereas, in the Hebrew text, it's not mentioned. Esther is also the only text in the Old Testament to take place exclusively in diaspora, in ancient Persia. All the other biblical texts take place, at least partially, on the land of Israel. I made a transposition: I took this sanctified story of diaspora and transposed it entirely into the reality and landscape of Israel. I also made some architectural cuts: I decided that all the interiors of the city would be filmed in Wadi Salib, a neighborhood in my hometown, Haifa, a place charged with meanings and memories, while the exteriors, the city walls, would be shot in Saint-Jean d'Acre. By creating a composite city whose winding streets are in Wadi Salib, I attempted to capture the contemporary memory of a predominantly Arab and Muslim neighborhood that is now being destroyed. Cinema will also create a visual record of this neighborhood that the current city of Haifa would like to see disappear, to erase its existence from our memory.

Different layers, different meanings.

III

Esther was filmed in Hebrew and Arabic, *Golem, the Spirit of Exile* (1992) was filmed in Paris, mainly in French, and *Berlin–Jerusalem* (1989) in Hebrew and German, which has a completely different significance. What connects all three of them is the reference to the text.

I often include excerpts from literary texts in my films. It's not adaptation. It's the question of interpretation that interests me, to borrow the French expression used for actors, *interprété par* (interpreted by). It involves, in a good Talmudic spirit, confronting old meanings and creating new ones, reinforcing memory, exposing contradictions—all of which are forms of interpretation.

In a poetic construction of cinema, imagery doesn't serve to illustrate. It's more of an exclamation point, a question mark, or irony. I like these tools that allow for this. This is also one of the reasons why I love long takes: for their sense of time and rhythm which differs from that of premeditated, cliché-ridden classical editing. I prefer the irregularity of long takes.

Another form, another choreography.

I believe that theological texts—or better said, archaic texts, for as a nonbeliever, I don't automatically attribute divine nature to them—are very ancient texts that manage to encode and decode human reflections that are still valid to this day. It's very moving for me, this great wisdom and observation of human nature from a time when we didn't have all these technological gadgets, all these machines that surround us today and to which we attribute the ability to encode and analyze human feelings.

These are the very first reflections of humanity transcribed by an alphabet at the beginning of the Iron Age. They are still relevant today with regard to ethics, desire, human nature, narrative form, etc. So why consider them as old texts only stamped by religion? If we do, they become no longer valid for us. Why not use cinema, which is a much newer medium, to reinterpret them? Anyway, I am not a professional filmmaker, so I can ask these kinds of questions.

In this exile trilogy, I immediately rule out the option of a naturalistic cinema that doesn't interest me, while seeking to expand the territory I give myself. Not encroaching on the territory of documentary but taking a step back from fiction.
My three films on the theme of the Golem, *Birth of a Golem* (1990), *Spirit of Exile* (1992), and *Petrified Garden* (1993), are like notebooks derived from texts that allow me to look at European or Russian society and understand something about racism in French society, for example. I transpose an archaic text that has no connection with the racist attitude of a part of French society and construct a sort of parable. This is my way of looking at a text whose origin I know, uprooting it, and transposing it into another reality that I know less because I am a foreigner. And I use my observations and my experience as a foreigner to build a disturbing parable about this society.

Strangely, I see a link between *Golem, the Spirit of Exile* and the first part of *Disengagement* (2007). These two films both transpose contemporary experience into meta-historical terms and give a musical value, a cinematic beauty, to a relatively frightening void. They carry a sort of threat in their non-naturalistic, non-illustrative character concerning Europe. *Disengagement*, for example, evokes a form of male impotence that creates a form of female hysteria. The brother's impotence. In a calm, lucid, almost authoritative manner, like in a religious ceremony, these films say: this is how I see you. These scenes disturb. And people resist. It's very disturbing to apply the text taken from the Book of Samuel about David and Goliath to the European situation, as at the beginning of *Spirit of Exile*, or the biblical discourse against injustice and exploitation of the poor and the denial of their history. These are strong stories. Unlike the Middle East, where conflicts are more apparent and visible, these currents are more repressed in European societies, they become like embers. In the first part of *Disengagement*, even aesthetically, I was aware of continuing a work started fifteen years ago with *Spirit of Exile*. And I continue by using this story as a pretext. Through its non-naturalistic treatment, the European landscape becomes like a cage that traps the female character. And the boy coming from Israel can only be out of place in this landscape, as if he were an extra.

Kadosh (1999) doesn't belong to this group because it's a film about a traditional society. It doesn't focus on a religious text. This story of two sisters is inspired by the very ambiguous observation of religious ritual. There's something intriguing to me about how it closes in on itself and claims to know the absolute truth, which is why it rejects any other proposition. In a sense, the arrogance with which the ultra-religious reject modernity is almost touching. It produces a different rhythm. And that's also why I dislike this elitism, this notion of absolute truth, this arrogance towards modernity, and this false sense of superiority. As an Israeli citizen, I don't want fundamentalism to gain ground, so I assert my viewpoint, as I did in *House* and *Field Diary* on the Israeli–Palestinian conflict, or in other films on different subjects.
It's in *Esther* and especially in *Golem, the Spirit of Exile* that the text allows me to create strangeness/alienation and attempt a mythical reading of the present. The presence of the Jewish–Arab conflict in *Esther* immediately disturbed Israelis, just as *Spirit of Exile* immediately provoked great hostility in Europe.

It's complex because it's also due to the combinatory nature of the text, which is a principle of Kabbalah.

IV

Take dust from a mountain, from untouched soil, and spread it throughout the house, and wash your body. From this pure dust, create a Golem, the creature you wish to form and animate, and above each limb, pronounce the consonant assigned to it in the* Sefer Yetzirah, *combining them with the consonants and vowels of the name of God.

What interested me at the outset of my trilogy on the Golem is that it's a very modern mythology that deals with the relationships between humans, or humanity, and the manufactured product.

Juliette Binoche in *Disengagement* (2007), a film inspired by *The Man Without Qualities*, by Robert Musil

What does the myth of the Golem say if we strip it of the story itself and the fable?

A man goes to the riverbank. He has all sorts of problems in his life and in his community. He must face his enemies. There is misery, economic problems, etc.

Like the Jews who have been living in the diaspora for centuries.

So, to face this situation, he goes to the riverbank because he wants to practice a kind of magic . . .

It is a kind of composition, a combination, to use mathematical vocabulary, to create an artificial being capable of combating nature, enemies, hatred, misery, and everything else. In a sense, it's the basis of civilization: since the Iron Age, humans have been looking for tools to control nature, to cultivate fields not only when it rains but also whenever they want, to extend their reach and enable them to fight their enemies, build houses, and provide themselves with shelter, etc.
So the myth of the Golem is essentially about the process of creating a manufactured object and the very complex dialectical relationship that is established between the human being and the artificial being that they build.

In a way, these films around the figure of the Golem and those on multinational corporations are films I made about a phenomenon that hadn't yet been named. The term "globalization" only came later. The last part of the Golem trilogy, *Petrified Garden*, deals with the Soviet Union as a kind of Golem.
What does that mean? That it's an idea. A human idea. Totalitarian communism builds a regime and, like the Golem, this construct collapses on humanity. That's the impression I had in Leningrad, in front of those huge dams that were being built to block rivers and were then abandoned mid-construction after creating major ecological disasters, diverting rivers, etc. So the USSR is a kind of Golem.

Returning to mythology, in this sense, *Golem, the Spirit of Exile* is a continuation of *Esther*: they are parables. So, the story of the Golem, quite simply:

This man goes to the riverbank. He makes the composition, the kabbalistic combination of words, meanings, letters, and manages to create an artificial being . . .

A robot. Frankenstein. They were all influenced by this myth of the Golem.

And this artificial being will help him with his manual tasks . . .

Like any machine. But of course, since we're in a Jewish story, it's necessary that . . .

Every Friday evening . . .

Even what makes the Golem function is very interesting because . . .

It's a piece of paper on which the name of God is written, and he places it in the Golem's mouth. And every Friday evening, he removes the piece of paper so that the Golem can rest during Shabbat.

It's very important: it's like an electronic card or a computer of that time. Even this idea—this thing, this gadget—that a text is needed to activate the Golem[1] is incredible: the earliest known version of the Golem dates back to the third century! It's an extraordinarily interesting story.

So one Friday evening, he forgets . . .

1 In the 1950s, Gershom Scholem, who had corresponded extensively with Walter Benjamin about Kabbalah texts, was asked to inaugurate the commissioning of a computer in Israel. Scholem agreed on the condition that the computer be called Golem.

I love this idea of forgetting. Of chance . . . It's human nature, something that isn't premeditated, not entirely programmed.

One evening, one Friday evening, he forgets to remove the piece of paper, and the Golem becomes uncontrollable. It starts destroying everything, setting fire to the community, going on a rampage . . .

Again, it's our relationship with technology, ecological disasters, and all these very sophisticated machines that we, human beings, have created and that end up destroying humanity. They will suffocate us if we don't manage to remove the card or the piece of paper from the mouth at the right moment. And even here, there are two versions of the end of the Golem's story. In one,

Finally, the rabbi manages to remove the piece of paper. On this piece of paper, which he slips into the Golem's mouth every Friday evening, is written, according to this ancient story, the word "emet," which means "truth." But when he manages to pull out the piece of paper, he only succeeds in removing the "e," leaving "met," which means "death."

Even the play on words. It's truly a beautiful story.

So the Golem collapses and kills him in its fall.

Which means that the artificial being will destroy humanity. And then version B:

He manages to remove the piece of paper and calm the Golem.

The story has always offered these two final versions, never wanting to provide the solution. Will humanity ultimately take control of the artificial being, this Golem that it created, or will the Golem collapse? Perhaps the Golem will cease to function, but at the cost of humanity's death?

opposite page
Pineapple (Ananas) (1983), a metaphor for the economics of multinational corporations and the structures that oppress the individual

The question posed by the Golem is fascinating, and it's no coincidence that I worked on it in parallel with *Pineapple (Ananas)* and *Bangkok–Bahrein*, two films that offer a global vision, not just a Jewish story.

By taking the legend surrounding the Golem as a starting point and bringing it to Paris or Russia, I don't just address this European reality. I blend it. This question is at the heart of *Golem, the Spirit of Exile*. The film also draws on the biblical Book of Ruth. It's a very interesting story because it emphasizes the origins of the most famous Jewish royal house, that of David. David's great-grandmother, Ruth, wasn't Jewish. She was a Moabite. She came to Israel only out of affection for Naomi, her mother-in-law. And the Old Testament includes her . . . It legitimizes this blending of cultures and the non-purist way in which the kingdom was created.
All these elements interest me, as does the fact that there are many versions of the Golem legend: that of Gustav Meyrink, the one called the "Litvak" version, the one in the Bible, the one from the Kabbalah book *Sefer Yetzirah*, the Book of Creation.

V

I went to the Bibliothèque Publique d'Information, at Beaubourg, to photocopy them and start working. I found all sorts of sketches on how to create a Golem. In a very ancient text about the first twelve hours of his existence, Adam is even called a Golem.

In the first hour, the earth was gathered
In the second hour, his form was created
In the third hour, he became a golem
In the fourth hour, his limbs were extended
In the fifth hour, his eyes opened
In the sixth hour, he received his soul
In the seventh hour, he stood on his feet

In the eighth hour, Eve was added to him
In the ninth hour, he was taken to Paradise
In the tenth hour, he learned of the prohibition
In the eleventh hour, he disobeyed
In the twelfth hour, he was expelled from Paradise.

For those who are true filmmakers, this kind of project must seem very strange because it's not really a film; there's no plot, much less a "pitch" . . . It's a project. I'd even say an artistic project, without the heavy connotation of that word, an artistic project in the sense that the question of cinema must emerge from the project itself. The initial idea is somehow freed from the subject. And this is true in almost all my films. As I'm interested in reflecting on this subject, I place a point in space, almost graphically, and tell my brain that I want to talk about this point. Why? I don't know.
It takes time. Then, I try to figure out, in different ways, why I'm interested in thinking about this point. Maybe because it's familiar to me, because it tells me something, although I'm not exactly sure what.
What links *Golem, the Spirit of Exile* to *Berlin–Jerusalem* is perhaps the extensive work done by the Germans on the Golem before the war. The most accomplished film, and perhaps the best known in German expressionist cinema, was Paul Wegener's in the 1920s. Wegener, who played the lead role in a Jewish story, that of the Golem, later became a Nazi actor. He himself became a Golem, in a way.[2]
I'm not surprised that all of this started in Germany because the Germans, particularly in Berlin, had experienced the impact of rapid urbanization and the industrial revolution more than any other city. In London, the industrial revolution had taken place earlier. In Paris, due to the very rigid plan imposed by Haussmann, the city was already designed. But Berlin only experienced rapid urbanization at the beginning of the twentieth century, as evidenced by its fractured form. To me, the shapes of cities are very significant. Paris, for example, is not a modern city. In

2 *The Golem* (1914) and *The Golem: How He Came into the World* (1920). We also find the influence of the Golem in *The Treasure* (1923), by Pabst, and in Lang's first *Mabuse* (1922).

France, the city admires and protects the architectural forms of the past and accepts the twentieth or twenty-first century only very subtly. This explains the conservative nature of the French, even though they've contributed to some very radical intellectual movements. And Berlin, because of its fractured nature, becomes a very interesting base for people coming from all over Europe. Due to its geographical location, it receives influences from Eastern Europe, Russia, Jewish influences, the Netherlands, Mies van der Rohe, Moholy-Nagy, Hungary . . . It's a true melting pot that then feels the need for a myth. One of the myths sought out by the expressionists is that of the Golem, a story that had been dormant for hundreds of years and found new meaning in modernity.
Like with *Berlin–Jerusalem* and *Birth of a Golem*, during that time I mainly lived in Europe and looked for themes and materials with which I could maintain this ambiguous relationship with the Israeli question that interests me. Feeling in tune and at the same time distant. And it's no coincidence that the last part of my Golem-themed trilogy, *Petrified Garden,* ends in Jaffa, as that's where two films of my next trilogy, *Devarim* (1995) and *Kadosh*, were filmed. It's the moment when I returned to live in Israel.

VI

Some elements frequently recur in my films: certain pieces of music, certain dialogues, certain texts . . . Others are less apparent, even if they are just as present. There is an obsessive dimension in every work. It exists in Andy Warhol, Cézanne, Joyce, Bach . . .
Within this obsession, a figure—the creator—tries, using the tools of their chosen medium, to establish a language capable of encoding what will be repeated from time to time in an infinite number of variations, or at least a very large number of variations, and listening. I speak of listening even if it's about painting or literature, listening to the effect produced by this particular ingredient. For instance, if I return to my films,

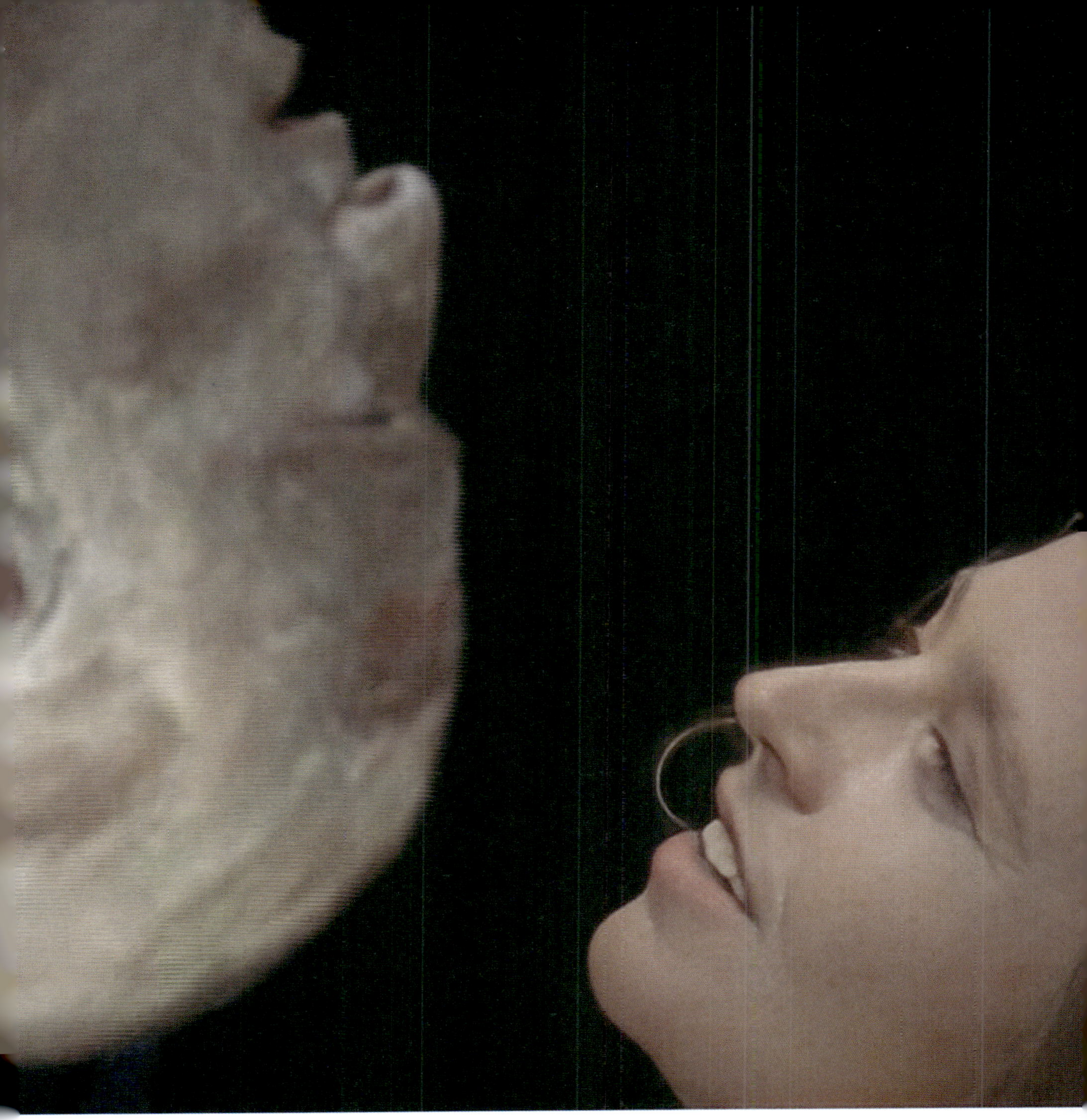

Vittorio Mezzogiorno and Hanna Schygulla in *Golem, the Spirit of Exile* (1991).
The Golem as a contemporary figure of exile and wanderer

there are sounds, music, texts, images. And, like in a chemical experiment, the creator observes the impact of an element they intimately understand on the general terms of the equation.

If we compare a film, a painting, a piece of writing, or a musical composition to a mathematical equation made up of different variables that are exchanged, modulated, emphasized, attenuated, euphemized, confronted with unknown, surprising elements, thematic questions, in this very large general equation that lasts roughly ninety minutes to two hours, the variables dance around one another, permutate, and create new meanings. Some elements are constants: these fixed, sometimes repetitive, elements are questioned by how they are placed in a new context.

Some elements continuously resurface, leaving traces again and again, and their very repetition gives a certain color, a certain connotation, but situated differently.

For example, the passage from Ecclesiastes, "There is a time for everything, and a season for every activity under the heavens," sung by Hanna Schygulla in *Spirit of Exile*, is heard in the last shot of *The Arena of Murder* (1996), when a car slowly turns around Yitzhak Rabin Square, where the Prime Minister was assassinated. This archaic meditation allows me to pose questions about the very site of a murder that carries historical and political significance. The same text is cited for the first time in *Metamorphosis of a Melody* (1992). In *The War of the Sons of Light Against the Sons of Darkness* (1993), it is associated with other archaic texts, while in *Kippur: War Memories* (1997) it resurfaces, as it does later in *Promised Land* (2004), where Hanna Schygulla recites it at the moment of a bomb explosion.

In many cases, this text is connected, for me, to Israel and the question of constructing a utopian image.

In *Berlin–Jerusalem*, this utopian image is a political and social concept embodied by Manya Shohat and Else Lasker-Schüler, the great German–Jewish expressionist poet. It's a film that presents a sort of iconoclastic, poetic transformation of Berlin in a strange blend with Jerusalem. One cannot address the issue of Israel without seeing this constant juxtaposition between the utopian image of Israel, whether modern or religious and political—Judea, that particular territory and what it represents in the history of humanity—and contemporary events. There is always this discrepancy, this tension between the territory and the project . . . or rather the mental projections of people onto this territory.

VII

Powerful films perhaps only begin after the screening ends. Cinema is an art that lies within a rather strange configuration. Films are often shown in fairly unattractive places where the seating isn't very comfortable and the projection conditions are far from ideal. Yet, when darkness falls and the screening starts, for the next hour and a half or two, we enter another universe of images, sounds, texts and dialogues, faces, and spectacle.

When the event ends and the lights come back on, we find ourselves returning to this rather unappealing building. Unlike sculpture, painting, or even a book, which leave behind a trace, an object, the film leaves no concrete trace behind.

Only a memory, an impression. Just an impression in our mind. There's nothing to take with you.

A highly abstract art that only exists as it's reproduced, because it's fundamentally about the reproduction of images of people, landscapes, sounds, and voices. In a sense, a film doesn't have the aura or uniqueness of an object, a sculpture, a painting, or a manuscript.

Often, in my films, the opening scene is, to use architectural terms, like an airlock, a foyer, a place where one settles to reflect on the space they've just left—such as the ticket counter where they bought their ticket, or the traffic jam they passed through before arriving. It allows one to understand that they're entering another space—a different mental, auditory, and iconographic space.

It's a deliberate act of separation between the experience we've just had and the one we're about to live.

Whether it's *Esther, Berlin–Jerusalem*, the *Golems*, the cities trilogy, the borders trilogy, *Kedma, Kippur, Eden,* or *Disengagement*, the opening scene allows for a separation between a before and an after.
The final shot is the last moment before the lights come back on in the theater, it is the last chance to say something, ask a question, or prolong an atmosphere or sensation that the film has tried to build. Sometimes, it's almost as if I wanted the film to continue, to be more explicit, or to provide the key to the enigma—the answers to the questions raised, whether visual, aesthetic, formal, thematic, or political. Most of my films offer this open ending, as if to refuse any definitive reading, happy or not, of the film.
In *Esther*, the film strictly adheres to the biblical text. So after setting up a certain décor throughout the film, the ruins of Wadi Salib, after building an iconography inspired by Persian miniatures with the lighting of Henri Alekan, and after borrowing monologues and texts from the Bible, I wanted, in a final gesture, to affirm the origins of my actors and incorporate them into the film. Because at that late stage, they could allow me to retrospectively shed a different light on certain elements of the film, as if to add another layer of interpretation to the Megillah, the scroll of Esther. Who are these actors? First, Simone Benyamini: born in the city of Beersheba, Israel, of Iraqi and Moroccan descent, she later moved north, and what struck her was the light and the sun in this country. And then Shmuel Wolf: born in Hungary, deported with his family, he arrived in Israel in 1949 and had to learn a new language—this is the story of *Kedma* that I would later film—and he is the narrator in the film. The eunuch Hatac is played by David Cohen the Oriental. Born in Alexandria, he was considered a Jew all his youth, but when he arrived in Israel, he was mistaken for an Arab and perceived as a pariah of society, just like the eunuchs were. Juliano Mer-Khamis is the son of a Palestinian and a Jew, both political figures who made their private lives a gesture of reconciliation—and the question remains open: Did they succeed? The son of a mixed marriage, representing the coexistence (or non-coexistence) of Jews and Arabs in the couple, he plays the role of the villain Haman. And Mohammad

Bakri, the great Palestinian actor who was born in Baana, Galilee, plays the traditional role of the Jew Mordecai. Together, they form one of the possible puzzles of Israeli reality. I thought it would be a mistake to end a film that serves as a parable without referring to the contemporary context and to how each of us is part of a human landscape. In this final shot, the actors' biographies become an integral part of the film's multiple meanings: they are useful questions rather than the key to interpretation. And all of this is put together in a very long nine-minute-and-thirty-eight-second sequence shot that brings together the ruins of this neighborhood, the actors' faces, and their autobiographical stories. Like an unwritten chapter of Esther. And I also claim the legitimacy of this modern interpretation of this archaic text. It seems to me that those who have never read Esther or Ruth will discover something of the rhythm, the profound beauty, the minimalism, and the ethical questions posed by this text.

Berlin–Jerusalem (1989). Scene of the burning of books viewed as being subversive or as representing ideologies opposed to Nazism in Berlin, in 1933. Lisa Kreuzer plays the German expressionist poet Else Lasker-Schüler

Pietà

Art and reciprocity

Stefano Boeri

In March 2021 I had Covid, and—while being in the hospital dealing with the cruelty of a pandemic that continued to affect many of our dearest loved ones—I thought back to a statue that was important to a part of my life, which was also locked in a hospital, on the other side of Milan.

It is a statue with which I had an almost daily relationship a few years ago, when I was the Culture Councilor of the City of Milan: Michelangelo Buonarroti's *Rondanini Pietà*.

Also, because it was my decision to relocate it to that hospital, in the center of Castello Sforzesco—the former military hospital during the Spanish domination.

While it is true that *hospital*, *suffering*, and *loneliness* have become words loaded with new meanings and images since the beginning of the Covid pandemic, I could not help but remember that it was precisely the *Rondanini Pietà* that had made me see in a new light words, concepts and feelings that had come back into focus with the epidemic: the word *old*, but also *care*, *solidarity*, *plague*, *pity*, and of course, *death*, *grief*, *reciprocity*, *missed burials* . . .

Michelangelo was 89 years old and a lonely elderly man when, on his deathbed, he left his last *Pietà* unfinished, despite having worked on it for more than 20 years.

The *Rondanini Pietà* is Michelangelo's third *Pietà*. The first extraordinary and movingly beautiful *Pietà* is in Rome, in St. Peter's Basilica, where Michelangelo, in his early twenties, sculpted a very young Madonna who appears to be the same age as her dead son.

opposite page
Michelangelo Buonarroti (1475–1564),
Rondanini Pietà, 1552–64

The second one, the *Bandini Pietà*, is in Florence, in the Museo dell'Opera del Duomo, and depicts the body of Christ supported not only by the Madonna but also by Mary Magdalene and Nicodemus, which for many interpreters is a self-representation of Michelangelo himself in his seventies, taking part in the deposition.

The third *Pietà*, the *Rondanini Pietà* is dated between 1552 and 1564, the year of Michelangelo's death.
It is said that Michelangelo sculpted it thinking of his own grave; he was certainly still working on it, in his Roman home, in the last days of his life. Michelangelo never completed his last *Pietà*, which remains unfinished, unhewn.
And it is precisely because of its incompleteness that this piece of white marble, from which the figure of the mother supporting her dead son emerges, has been emanating a unique and special power for 450 years.

Unlike the first two *Pietàs*, the *Rondanini Pietà* is a timeless work, almost appearing like a contemporary sculpture—a twentieth-century cubist or expressionist piece of art.
But there's more: it is a work open to multiple interpretations, which changes its meaning depending on how you look at it; and, in order to understand it, one has to walk around it.
It's no coincidence that artists like Alberto Giacometti or Henry Moore, who worked on unfinished forms, helped us discover it, describing a work that is extraordinary precisely because it is "disunited" between the lower part, in the anatomical realist style, and the upper part, dictated by emotionality and the thought of death. It is extraordinary because it is able to unite multiple interpretations in one piece of marble.

The truth is that for us to understand its value, the *Rondanini Pietà* had to wait almost four centuries.
The *Pietà* was left, almost abandoned, in the courtyard of a Count's private palace in Rome, after which the sculpture took its name.
In 1952, thanks to the great Fernanda Wittgens, Director of the Pinaco-

teca di Brera, the Municipality of Milan purchased it, raising the 150 million lire needed through public fundraising among citizens. The *Rondanini Pietà* therefore belongs to all Milanese citizens. For this reason, in 2011, when I took office as the Culture Councilor in Milan, I sought to understand how that statue, purchased with great generosity by the Milanese people, could once again become accessible to the experience and memory of all the citizens and visitors in Milan.

Once purchased from Rome, the *Rondanini Pietà* was brought to the Scarioni Room, the last room of the Lombard Renaissance Museum at Castello Sforzesco. The young and talented architects in charge of its set up, the BBPR group, who would later become famous for designing the Velasca Tower in Milan, were likely aware that it was a sculpture that is difficult to decipher and entirely different from the Lombard art tradition. They decided to place it, perhaps with the intent of protecting it, behind an elegant slate backdrop where, hidden and to the substantial indifference of the Milanese people, it remained for 50 years.

Its placement was, in fact, not easily accessible to everyone, at the bottom of a long staircase. Additionally, the statue was essentially invisible at first glance, and even once discovered, it was impossible to walk around it and gain the proper distance to fully appreciate it.

Encouraged by the expert opinion of art historian Giovanni Agosti, I decided to attempt relocating the *Pietà* to another part of the Castello Sforzesco.
I was convinced that if it remained behind that elegant slate backdrop, not only would few people see it, but more importantly, there was not enough physical space to walk around it and fully experience the powerful energy the sculpture exudes.
We needed to find a more suitable space.

Then, a miracle happened.
On a cold December morning in 2012, while Agosti, Castle Director

Claudio Salsi, art conservator Giovanna Mori and I were searching for a new location for the *Pietà*, we unexpectedly discovered an astonishing space: a place that had been used as a warehouse for decades and had never been restored.
It was the former Hospital room where dying Spanish soldiers were brought during the plague of St. Charles.
The room had remained untouched for 450 years, with Spanish insignia still frescoed on the walls and the words of the *Credo*, the prayer recited at the moment of death, on the ceiling.
It was a place, created in the same years as the *Pietà* and dedicated to suffering and hope, where the sense of death and the sacred was still profoundly present.

We decided to test the place by bringing an ancient and beautiful plaster cast of the statue into that room.
It was surprising to finally see the *Rondanini Pietà* radiate its power from a space that seemed to have awaited its arrival for centuries.
Upon seeing the cast of the *Pietà* in the large former Hospital room, Luca Ronconi, the great theater director, uttered an unforgettable phrase: "It seems to have come here on its own."

In the same year, a highly complex negotiation began involving the mayor, the superintendent, conservators, the Opificio delle Pietre Dure, the National Institute of Restoration, the Ministry, the Curia, engineers, architects, technicians, legal experts, and even the Vatican.
Naturally, the opinion of the Milanese *intelligentsia*, largely reluctant to disregard the BBPR's concept, was also a factor.
The truth is, I never disregarded their project, which was elegant and intelligent for a work that was still largely incomprehensible to the public in the 1950s.
What I was convinced of was that in 2012, 50 years after the *Pietà* was purchased, thanks to a different sensitivity towards the unfinished nature of art and contemporary interpretations by figures like Henry Moore and Alda Merini, the *Pietà* finally deserved a different visibility.

Stefano Boeri and Bob Dylan visiting the *Rondanini Pietà*, 2013

To support the relocation of the statue, I decided to invite people and friends to see the cast of the *Pietà* in the new location. I cannot forget that some of them, like Lea Vergine and Enzo Mari, are no longer with us due to Covid-19. I like to think that the *Pietà*, now finally settled in the former Spanish Hospital, somehow contains and remembers them. In that room, the void that Milan feels is somewhat lessened.

One foggy evening, Bob Dylan came to see it as well. He was in Milan for an exhibition of his paintings, and we brought him to visit the *Pietà*. He remained silent for fifteen minutes.
That time spent next to Bob Dylan, hooded and alongside Michelangelo, was one of the most intense and surreal moments of my life.

As I mentioned, being unfinished and embodying multiple successive attempts by Michelangelo to transform the mother's embrace of her dead son into stone, the *Pietà* changes depending on the viewer's perspective. When viewed frontally, it is the mother supporting the son, who almost seems to slip beneath her body. But just by walking around it, it appears to be the son supporting the mother, who leans her face over him.
This movement of the two bodies fused in stone is both moving and miraculous. An artwork that asks the viewer to add meaning to its unfinished parts and voids is, in essence, an open work that initiates an exchange with those who look at it.

Michelangelo's miracle was to gift us, on the point of death, a sculpture that unites the concept of *pietà* with that of *reciprocity*.
It speaks not only of compassion but also of empathy, the projection of our gaze and feelings into the eyes of those who look at us, and the introjection of others' feelings into our view of the world.

With this broader concept of *pietà* as mutual attention in mind, in the early months of 2013, we began to think about where we should temporarily relocate the *Pietà* while the former Spanish Hospital was being restored. We considered the chapel in the panopticon at the center of the San Vittore prison, at the intersection of the six wings housing the inmates.

Imagine: bringing that concept of *pietà* into the panopticon would have not only drawn the world's attention, for once, to the condition of Italian prisons but would have also accomplished something even more significant.
By attracting the gazes of inmates, prison guards, relatives, and visitors who we anticipated could visit the statue at certain times, the *Rondanini Pietà* would have been at the center of an intense variety of attentions and perspectives, all directed towards the central panoptic space of the chapel—a space originally intended for observing and controlling the lives of prisoners.
Michelangelo's *Pietà* would have reversed the very meaning of prison life and, I believe, allowed those confined to incarceration to free their thoughts.

However, if the transfer from one room to another within Castello Sforzesco was highly complicated, planning to move it to a prison, even if only for a few months, was even more so.

In addition to the countless authorizations, stamps, and permissions required, along with consultations with people and institutions, there was political controversy: one of the most prominent voices was an art curator, Vittorio Sgarbi, who, in a meeting at the Architects' Association, told me that it was pointless to bring Michelangelo's *Pietà* to a place where the majority of inmates are Muslim and thus would never understand the statue.

Nonetheless, I remained convinced that our municipal administration, the first left-wing administration in Milan in over 20 years, would have understood that this was neither a provocative gesture nor a utopia, but rather and above all, a project of inclusion within the city's daily life for a minority—the inmates of San Vittore—who also deserved attention.

In the end, we obtained nearly all the necessary administrative requirements, including those from the Director of the Circondariale prison, the Superintendency, the Ministry, and the Opificio delle Pietre Dure.

But just then, my life unexpectedly changed.
Due to disagreements with the Mayor, I had to cease my role as alderman much earlier than expected. As a result, despite having laid the groundwork for the relocation of the *Rondanini Pietà* to its new museum within Castello Sforzesco, I was unable to carry out the most visionary and passionate part of that project: overturning the very concept of prison suffering through an extraordinary work of art.

Bringing the *Rondanini Pietà* into the prison, bringing consolation to that place of pain, was the most important project of my brief political career. Perhaps one of the most important projects of my life.
Its failure, as often happens with failures born from radical ideas, was both a great sorrow and a great lesson.

following pages
Michelangelo Buonarroti (1475–1564),
Rondanini Pietà, 1552–64

Kippur (2000)

War Requiem

Meeting death on Yom Kippur

Amos Gitai

Writers can write texts
scientists can present data
What options do filmmakers have?
The cinema I make requires time
and space
a rhythm.
It has to stretch out the time unit
to counter the media system,
almost in a subversive manner
its aim is to humanize the other
and this takes time.

We must embrace contradictions
and take the time to "arrange"
space,
rhythm,
discourse,
speech,
music,
sounds,
noises,
silence.

What is the meaning of the word
Requiem

It's a lament to put to rest
the souls of the dead

We were seven
who left Ramat David airbase
in the early hours of
October 11
Avner Hacohen
Gadi Klein
Nadav Gottlieb
Dr. Zeev Klein
Tsaki Tzuriel
Uzi Cantoni
and myself
Only six came back
Gadi did not
Dr. Zeev Klein died soon after.

All the others still keep
bodily and mental wounds

When she agreed to work with me,
Jeanne Moreau said,
“Amos, I only work on films when
I think I will learn something
I didn’t already know.”

So, when Mira Lapidot suggested that
I should write a text relating
to the exhibition
that we are opening at the
Tel Aviv Museum of Art,
I said to myself that this
reinvestigation of the event

that happened fifty years ago
(perhaps even scratching again
the old wounds)
will teach me something.
This revisiting presents an occasion
for deeper learning.

What did I learn again now?
What does the transposition
of this event into
an exhibition show me again.

I can see again
that the camera had served as a shield.
The camera acted as
a chronicler of our times.
In this sense, it's the modern fetish
par excellence.

In October 1973,
when I was an architecture student,
my mother gave me a Super8 camera,
as a birthday present.
During the war,
I took this camera with me and recorded
what I saw from the helicopter:
faces, the texture of the earth,
bits of rescue missions,
and so on.
Paradoxically, it was all quite abstract.
But I didn't take the camera with me
the day my rescue helicopter

was shot down
by a Syrian missile.
I had left it behind at the airbase,
and this is why
the short Super8 films I made
during the war
still exist today
and can be shown in the exhibition.
After all, this little camera is an object
that has helped me immensely.

How?

It has been a filter,
keeping traces of memories
by recording events in real-time,
as well as a shield between the real
and myself.
I used the camera to document
events
as they were happening
and this activity required distance.

The camera was this instrument
of distancing.
In a certain way,
it shielded my soul from the war.

The camera makes it possible,
on the one hand,
to document and conserve memory
– if we speak about war

Kippur (2000). A Syrian missile has just hit the helicopter Amos Gitai and the members of his rescue crew unit were in

where death and loss are real possibilities.
On the other, the moment you pick up
the camera,
you become an outsider.

One can also say that
the camera is a kind of a weapon,
a kind of fetish embodying
my distancing from society.
It's for this reason that
I have an affective relationship
with the medium of cinema.

Bertolt Brecht spoke of distancing
as a kind of
basic condition of any creation.
From an optical standpoint,
we know that objects seen from
too close loose clarity.
We need some distance
to see
and the camera is a tool that helps
to create this distance.
It's an object that places you
outside the group
that you are about to film.
Part of me wanted to belong
to a group.
That is what landed me
in a rescue helicopter
during the Yom Kippur War.
Another part of me never

really wanted to be part of this group
in an Israeli society that demands
total adherence to a collective project.

A small group of seven people
found itself in a Bell 205 helicopter
flying into Syrian territory
to try and rescue
Schneider,
a Skyhawk pilot
whose jet had been shot down
by the Syrians.

Mira suggested that,
as an introduction to the exhibition
Kippur: War Requiem,
she would present portraits
of these seven men

The Yom Kippur War started
on October 6, 1973.
The weather was fair,
a mix of sun and clouds,
it was silent like any other Kippur Day
and then at 2 p.m.,
the sirens suddenly started howling.
The country descended into chaos.
Like others, I felt compelled
to defend the country.
I called my friend Uzi
and we went to look for the war.
But in all the chaos,

Opening scene of *Kippur* (2000)

we couldn't find our unit
and we ended up joining
an airborne rescue team.

The keyword of what I just wrote is
Chaos
and my intention, in my part
of this exhibition,
is to instill the sensation of
Chaos.
A continuous rupture
in which only the juxtaposition of
fragments of
memories
traces of object
sounds and noises
can attempt to recompose this sensation

On October 11,
on the fifth day of the war,
our helicopter was shot down
by a Syrian missile.
The cockpit exploded
and Gadi the copilot was
decapitated.
Avner, the first pilot, managed to fly
for three more minutes
and then we crashed
behind Israeli lines.
The event itself was quite short,
but it was nevertheless an encounter
with death.

For me, the most shocking event
of this war
occurred before we were shot down.
I had just put an oxygen tube
in the mouth of a seriously wounded
colonel,
and we were flying to the hospital.
At some point,
some notes he had jotted down
before the war fell out of his pocket.
I bent down to pick them up.
They were about buying tomatoes
at the market.
When I leaned up,
he was gone,
he had died.
The passage from life to death
had not been dramatic
at all
and that in itself is the real drama.

All of these elements
constitute biographical material
that is personal.
But how does one make a film
or an installation
out of it?
It's really an open question
that I will try
to answer through the exhibition itself
by using
the Super8 films

that I made during the war,
the drawings that I made
immediately after the crash
fifty years ago,
parts of my documentary film
War Memories
that I made twenty years after the war,
and the feature film *Kippur*
that I made 27 years after.

Sometimes I ask myself
why it took me
such a long lapse of time.
I think that
right after the war,
I wanted to forget.
I did not want to talk about it.
When the prospect of peace
started to appear
with the election of Yitzhak Rabin,
I decided that I would talk about the war
in a dialectical manner
to express the damage and destruction
of any war
to remind those
who wanted to go to the next war
what war is about:
The loss of the individual,
the waste of all resources.

I thought that there would
come a time when
war fatigue sets in.
And peace comes, not in dramatic fashion,
just as a conclusion
to the savagery.
Perhaps we will arrive at the same decision
the Europeans did
after two bloody and murderous
world wars
Understanding that they can
disagree and have disputes
But not shoot.

Right after the war,
and I cannot say exactly why,
I hung the uniform
I wore during the war
and I filmed it.
It was raining
the first rain after the war
I felt emotional
the globe was still turning
the cycles of nature were going on.

How does one materialize
an encounter with fate?
How does one give it form?
The true challenge is to make things
more abstract
not illustrative
when we read texts

our minds can roam freely
and dress the text
with different forms.
Cinema is instantly concrete.
It's me in the picture.
It's you.
How does one take a personal memory
and render its abstract quality
in a cinematic or an exhibition form?
How does one take an event
like the Yom Kippur War
and give it a universal value,
one that is beyond being
a traumatic Israeli event

Twenty years after the war
when I was filming
Efratia, my mother, sent me a note
with some questions and
exclamations marks
that I still find relevant.

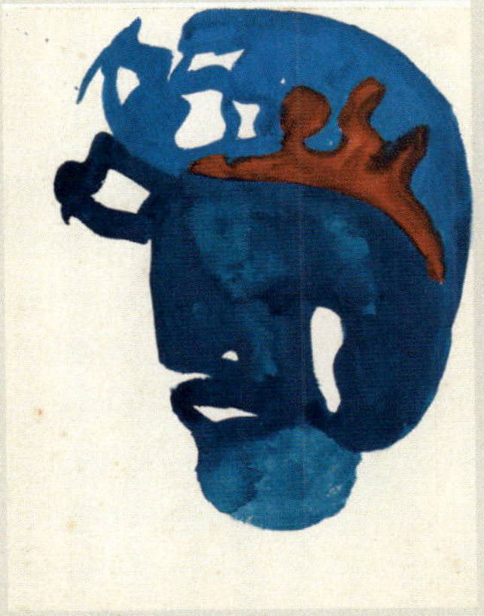

Drawing by Amos Gitai made after he was wounded during the Yom Kippur War (1973). Private collection

Here it is:

Haifa, October 11, 1994

My dear Amos; my very, very dear son!

I remember my childhood, my youth, so beautiful on the golden sands of little Tel Aviv; memories of love on those dunes . . . But at my age, one is more modest, shier than during youth. So many battles, challenges, intermittent studies. I'm still frustrated with those. A little university, but a feeling of gaps, and especially broken dreams, a crack that strains and strains . . . What will the future hold? Regarding your question about changing countries, I think about that sometimes, but where to go? No, I can't see any other place for me. After all, there are many things that make life good in Israel today: the beautiful Carmel, the seaside, and the boardwalk, which is so magnificent at nightfall, Dado beach, splendid sunsets, and the university. And there are the theaters in Haifa and Jerusalem. And the music. And the few friends who remain.
We know what friendship is.
For me, buried here are people of the generation of the Second Aliya and my parents, whom I'll never forget and will always love. Buried here are my dearest friends, my husband the architect, and many more. I don't visit cemeteries. No! Dry and hollow bones! But the memories are tied to this place, and it's difficult to uproot them. Only a few escapes abroad, and then the return.
For me, there is certainly no other place but worry gnaws at me: what will happen to you, the young, the flesh of our flesh, you who remain and live the fallen dream? Will you overcome the darkness that engulfs us?

Be well,
Mama

opposite page
Efratia Margalit Munschik Gitai,
Tel Aviv, Israel, 1928. Private collection

Multiplicity in collaboration with Giovanni Maria Bellu, *Solid Sea 01: the Ghost Ship*, 2002

Solid Sea

Mediterranean stories

Stefano Boeri

Mediterranean: A Cultural Landscape (1987) is perhaps the best-known text by Predrag Matvejević. Born in 1932 in Mostar, Matvejević was a professor at the Sorbonne in Paris and Sapienza in Rome. He was an important figure in international geopolitics, a defender of dissident intellectuals during the worst period of Soviet oppression, and a great advocate of the intellectual unity of Europe.

Matvejević's book is a kind of phenomenology of the Mediterranean. The first chapter is a breviary, the second a cartographic reconstruction, and the third a glossary. All invite us, from different perspectives, to explore the deep soul of a great inland sea that has been the cradle of some of the most extraordinary human civilizations for centuries.

"Matvejević's text," Claudio Magris tells us in the preface, "seems to embed culture and history into things. He tells us about harbors, islands, buoys, hemp ropes, waves, winds, deep currents, clouds, markets, prayers, and blasphemies, languages and wells, soils, smells, measurements, lighthouses, monasteries, fishermen, seagulls, rains, and civilization. As in the pages of Simenon's *Méditerranée en goélette* (Mediterranean in a Boat, 1934), also in *A Cultural Landscape* the Mediterranean seems to suddenly emerge from the depths of geography and imagination—in daily objects, in the wrinkles on men's faces, in the flavors of wine and oil, in the colors of the waves. It appears as a place of the soul as well as of geography, where routes were woven and built a common knowledge, where words and terms took shape that became recurrent in the languages and dialects of all its coasts and cities.

I cannot forget when, in 1996, Matvejević came to present his *Mediterranean: A Cultural Landscape* in Milan. Even then, his vision of the Mediter-

Solid Sea Legend

- the actual course of the *Yohan*
- the course of the *Yohan* as declared to the authorities
- overland travel of passengers before boarding the *Yohan*
- air travel of passengers before boarding the *Yohan*
- sea travel of passengers before boarding the *Yohan*

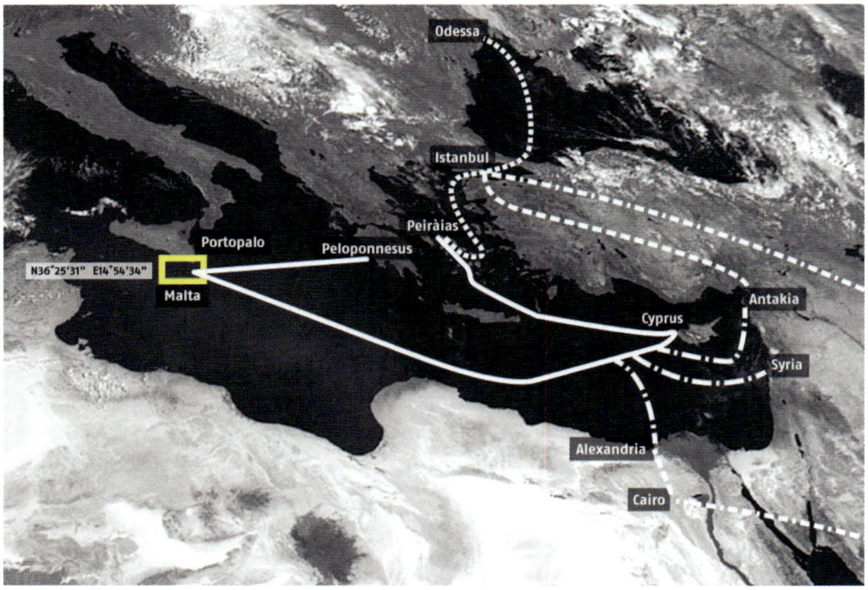

The tragic story of a shipwreck that occurred off the southern coast of Sicily on Christmas Eve 1996

Underwater images of *F174*'s shipwreck

ranean as the cradle of civilization, as a common matrix declined in all contextual differences—geography, religions, customs—was beginning to be challenged by dramatic news events. I remember in particular an event that became, for us at Multiplicity—a network of architects, photographers, researchers, and geographers that was being formed in those years—a catalyst for research that would later come to reinterpret the meaning and nature of the Mediterranean.

Multiplicity's work began with the reconstruction of a tragedy that occurred on Christmas Eve 1996, 20 miles off the coast of southeastern Sicily. A boat flying the Honduran flag, named *Yohan*, was carrying a large group of young Sinhalese refugees fleeing the civil war. While transferring the refugees onto a small Maltese wooden boat identified with the code F174 that was supposed to take them to the coast of Porto Palo, the two vessels collided. The small boat, loaded with people, quickly sank. The sea was very rough and the lifeboat went down immediately, causing the deaths of 283 men and women. But the ship, led by an Egyptian commander, drifted away without sending any emergency or distress signals. The few survivors of the tragedy, those who managed to climb back onto the ship thanks to the ropes thrown by the sailors, tried hard to summon rescue, to call for help, to report the serious incident to the Maltese, Italian and Greek coast guards. But for five years, the response was a terrible and constant silence. The tragedy was guiltily removed and remained hidden until 2001, despite fishermen in Porto Palo continued to find scraps of clothing and parts of the victims' bodies in deep-sea fishing nets. Journalist Giovanni Maria Bellu rented an underwater camera and was finally able to locate the exact spot where the sunken lifeboat was, with the remains of the bodies still held in the depths of the Mediterranean. The discovery of the identity card of a young Sinhalese by fisherman Salvatore Lupo finally brought the tragedy to light.

Today, stories like this are unfortunately common, but at the time—in the general silence—we at Multiplicity decided to carry out an investigation together with Bellu and make it public. We collected interviews with the

witnesses of that tragedy, including the ship's captain, the fishermen who had found the bodies of the victims, survivors, relatives, and the commanders of the Malta harbor master's office and the Sicilian harbor master's office in Porto Palo. With the help of Maddalena Bregani, Francesco Jodice, Maki Gherzi, Giovanni La Varra, Francisca Insulza, John Palmesino, and Paolo Vari, we reconstructed this story and, with the aim of keeping the memory alive, we proposed an art installation on it to Okwui Enwezor, then curator of Documenta 11 in Kassel, one of the most important contemporary art exhibitions.
Okwui left us a few years ago. He knew well how to address the big questions of geopolitics through the language of visual art; he understood that our research was highlighting a phenomenon, that of the illegal flows of immigration across the Mediterranean, which in time would take on biblical proportions.
Multiplicity's installation at Documenta 11, which opened in June 2002, consisted of two opposing screens: on the first, representing the time of the tragedy, a satellite image of the Mediterranean was projected with the route taken by the two boats and the geographical coordinates of their collision point on Christmas Eve. On the second, representing the space of the tragedy, an underwater camera video showed a tangle of clothes and remains of the victims' bodies at the bottom of the sea. In a second room we collected interviews with all the witnesses.

Today, those bodies are still at the bottom of the sea. That event has opened a wound that year after year has widened to become a chasm in the history, culture, and politics of our country, as well as in the conception of our inland sea. People began to understand that the Mediterranean was not simply a shared body of water bringing dialogue to the coastal cities of three continents, but was becoming something very different: a solid continent, traversed by rigid routes, divided by impassable barriers. And "Solid Sea" was the term we used to title our installation (*Solid Sea.01: the Ghost Ship*, 2002).

Indeed, the solidification of this continent reflected the increasing specialization of the routes that ran through it. Fisherman, sailor, soldier, mi-

grant, tourist: whatever the identity of those who crossed it, it was channeled into an independent, rigid route that did not intersect with that of other navigators. This rigidity strongly clashed with what had been for centuries the lifeblood of the Mediterranean: the intersection of routes and flows, trade exchanges between ports, relations between cities, food cross-pollinations between coastal areas, and artistic and cultural contaminations between languages and traditions; always different but always facing—and thus embraced by—a common sea.
At the turn of the second millennium, an ancient tradition of exchanges was thus beginning to be frustrated, penalized, destroyed by the new nature of a sea that, from being a liquid and open cradle, had become a rigid projection of the conflicts of contemporary geopolitics. A change that could not but also have consequences for the life of the cities that constitute the living edges of this solid sea.

Matvejević's book was inspirational and pivotal in 2018 while we were working on the staging of Euripides' *The Trojan Women* for the great Greek theater in Syracuse; built in the fifth century B.C. in limestone, the theater has been left almost untouched since then, despite over two thousand years of history. Antonio Calbi, the Superintendent of the National Institute of Ancient Drama, asked me to design the set for the theatrical staging of the ancient Greek tragedy, directed by Muriel Mayette-Holtz.
I reacquainted myself with Euripides and his tragedy thanks to the famous adaptation that Sartre wrote at a time when the echo of the war in Algeria, which began in 1954 and ended with the African state's declaration of independence, was still very strong. It was a most violent conflict, during which France had measured the consequences of a long and aggressive colonial phase. A philosopher as attentive to politics as Sartre could not but reckon with that veritable civil war in those years, which had left hundreds of thousands of dead on the trenches and had been an occasion of shame for French nationalist policy. While respecting the text, Sartre proposed, therefore, an implicit and subtle updating of Euripides' tragedy. It was not unlike that which Euripides himself had accomplished twenty-four centuries earlier, when in Athens, in 415 B.C., with *The Trojan*

previous pages
The devastation of the Vaia Storm,
October 2018

The trees' journey from Friuli Venezia Giulia to Sicily

Women he implicitly staged the ongoing war in the Peloponnese, the aggression against Melos by the Athenians and the extermination of its population.

In *The Trojan Women*, reversing the Homeric and epic perspective of the war, Euripides narrates an affair that has neither losers nor victors through the voices of the women who survived the burning of Troy. With the city now destroyed by fire, the mothers, daughters, and sisters of the slain men approach the coast where the ships of the Achaeans await them to kidnap them and take them by force from Troy. The men are dead; one of the few children who had survived, Astyanax, the firstborn son of Andromache and Hector, is torn from his mother's arms and hurled by Achaean soldiers from the smouldering walls of Troy so that he could not avenge the killing of his father. Thus, the main characters are women who have lost everything, deprived of a future. Together with my colleague Anastasia Kucherova, who helped me conceive and create this set design, we held forth about the space of the Greek theater, coeval with Euripides' writing, and what was the best way to enhance Muriel Mayette-Holtz's direction, which focused essentially on the power of the words, voices, and bodies of the women chosen by Euripides as the absolute protagonists of the tragedy.

Other architects before me, including Rem Koolhaas and Massimiliano Fuksas, had been called to work on the Greek theater's stage in Syracuse. I am not a scenographer, and my intent, rather than to make a set with canvas wings and screens, was to create a landscape, or more accurately, to enhance the components of the very landscape of the Syracuse theater. I was looking for a scenic device that would make the voices of the actresses led by Mayette-Holtz resonate between the sixty-seven tiers of steps of the cavea and the forest of holm oaks and pines behind the stage, and that would best accommodate the movement of the actors.

And so, while I was reading the text of the tragedy and reflecting on the set design, it occurred to me to use, as the main protagonists of the theatrical scene, the trees destroyed by the Vaia Storm, which, at the end of October 2018, had felled about 14 million white and red firs in an area of 41 thou-

sand hectares, between the mountains of Trentino, Friuli, and Veneto. It was a sudden and extremely powerful storm, with a 200-kilometer-per-hour sirocco wind that had grafted on an unexpected weather disturbance, with continuous and roaring rain. The planting of a monocultural, fir-only forest with too high a density, together with excess water in the soil, had probably weakened the root hold and created a ripple effect that had uprooted or broken millions of trees in seconds. A most powerful and disturbing image, especially when we think of forests as witnesses to a centuries-old history.
In just a few weeks, thanks to the collaboration of the mayor of Sappada, a small city in Friuli, and other administrators from some of the towns most affected by the Vaia Storm, and with the support of INDA and the mayor of Syracuse, we were able to bring 500 fir trunks, between four and eight meters tall, to Syracuse from the mountains of Carnia. A short film directed by Stefano Santamato told the story of this dead wood's journey, first on a truck and then on a ship, to the port of Syracuse and to the theater workshops where the set was built.

The dead trees were arranged on the stage erect, as if they were the columns that survived the destruction of a temple. Called on to regain dignity, the fir trees stood in the middle, between the audience of humans and the audience of living trees, in the forest behind them.
For two months, this temple of worn trunks, worn down by storm and death, hosted the movement of the bodies of Trojan women and the screams of Hecuba, queen of Troy, of Polyxena, of Andromache.
This desperation is not unlike that of Syrian or Libyan or Ethiopian women, forced to flee the ongoing civil war or drought, to risk their lives and that of their children by crossing the Mediterranean to land on Sicilian shores, sometimes only a few kilometers from the Greek theater where we had staged Euripides' tragedy.
Plant nature, torn apart by an environmental catastrophe largely exacerbated by human action and the effects of global warming, had thus become the setting for a tragedy that lives out of time—human nature destroyed by war.

My knowledge of Mediterranean cities and the vibrant relationship between city and port was formed in Genoa.
Genoa, squeezed between the mountains and the sea, like many other Mediterranean cities, is a school. It is a city torn apart by conflicts and great imbalances in its social composition, which perhaps because of this has produced some extraordinary accelerations in the world of art, culture, and music. It is an untamed city, capable of rising up from accidents and great tragedies, not least the collapse of the Morandi Bridge.
In Genoa, and from Genoa, thanks to Giuliano Gallanti, president of the Port Authority, who invited me to coordinate the work of the master plan in 1994, I learned about Mediterranean ports: working in Marseille, Thessaloniki, Trieste, Naples, Cagliari, frequenting the docks of Beirut, Alexandria, Haifa, Istanbul, I experienced the vibrant history of cities born together with their port.

People often think of the port as being on the periphery of the mainland. Nothing could be more wrong: ship docks are ontologically a central place, where flows, carriers, goods, and people arriving from sea and land meet, intersect, create, and exchange spaces incessantly. Because of this centrality made up of constant movement, the historic ports of Mediterranean cities came into being (along with their cities) as mestizo places; through the presence of markets, housing for sailors, and *provveditorie*, they incorporated the variety, heterogeneity, and unpredictability of urban life.
In spite of decades of forced separation, which for many years pushed Mediterranean ports to turn their backs on their cities and follow autonomous development logics and procedures, on their docks, piers, warehouses, workshops, and repair docks, one can always find the sign of an ancient intermingling of lives, routes, and cultures.

After all, Mediterranean ports are necessarily places in constant and rapid transformation. They keep changing, sometimes even by choices made thousands of miles away: all it takes is for a shipowner to change the routes of his carriers, or for a new technology to take over in the transportation of goods.

Stefano Boeri Architetti, Stage design for Euripides' tragedy *The Trojan Women*, directed by Muriel Mayette-Holtz, lighting design by Angelo Linzalata, Greek theater, Syracuse, Italy, 2019

One of the most striking innovations occurred in the last century following the invention of containers: this very simple module changed and transfigured port operations worldwide, requiring large logistical areas to handle its volumes and challenging the historic ports and their system of piers, silos, and cranes for transporting bulk goods.
It is an endless story of mutations, deaths and rebirths. Even today, the enlargement of the Suez Canal and the construction of gigantic container ships are changing ship routes and thus the geopolitics of ports; just as in the near future global warming and the melting of portions of the Arctic ice cap may make it possible to circumnavigate part of the North Pole, effectively creating an alternative to the Suez route and upsetting the hierarchies and conditions of cargo traffic in the world.

The relationship between technological innovation, ports, routes, and docks is, in short, a fundamental key to understanding the history of the Mediterranean and its cities. After the powerful spreading of container technology and the creation, away from the historic ports, of the new large logistics platforms, the historic Mediterranean ports had been emptied of their role, closed in a self-referential logic.

A few years later, I was involved in a project for the Mediterranean Research Center in Marseille, Villa Méditerranée, strongly promoted by the former President of the Region, Michel Vauzelle. In 2004 we won an architectural competition for the project which, following a series of discussions among local administrations, would only be realized in 2013, on the occasion of Marseille being the European Capital of Culture. It is a work of architecture that I am very fond of, which, instead of having its back to the Mediterranean, as most of the public architecture built recently on its edges does, chose to open up to the sea and even house it within it.
Villa Méditerranée is a work of architecture on three levels: a tall horizontal volume cantilevered over a dock that houses a large flexible space; a vertical volume that contains administrative offices; and a volume built below the water level of the dock where a theater and a series of exhibition spaces are housed. Thanks to these three volumes arranged in a C-shape,

Boeri Studio, Villa Méditerranée, Marseille, France, 2013

Villa Méditerranée is a work of architecture that envelops and contains the sea. At its center, there is in fact a veritable water plaza: a dock connected to the Mediterranean thanks to a navigable canal, which is the fourth essential component of a project that is a political manifesto designed for a mestizo city full of intense cultural variations. The architectural design invokes the idea of a permeable sea again, toward which one can turn with an attitude of care and openness.
This project has been important in inspiring some of our subsequent projects: in particular that of the never fully completed construction of the Western Mediterranean maritime hub in the former Arsenal of La Maddalena, Sardinia.

Speaking of intertwining architecture and politics, I recall with emotion that in 2013, at the time of its inauguration, all the presidents of the Parliaments of the Mediterranean countries gathered in Villa Méditerranée, together with the presidents of the EU Parliaments. This is a memorable image of the potential of a politics that sometimes, unfortunately rarely, knows how to go beyond contingencies and look to the future.
Even today, confirming how architecture can sometimes miraculously survive radical transformations in their intended use, Villa Méditerranée has become the site of the philological reconstruction of an extraordinary cave near Marseille that houses rock paintings created between 33,000 and 19,000 years ago. Our architecture has not lost its power as a building open to the currents and flows of the Mediterranean.

But the Mediterranean is also an individual universe (as Giancarlo De Carlo tells us in his book, *Viaggi in Grecia*, 2010), an inland sea that has a territorial and geographical intimacy with the life trajectories of each of us. I don't think it is a coincidence that this intimacy has also been embodied in some residential, private, and sublime examples of architecture. Here are, very briefly, three of them.
The first, and best known, is certainly Curzio Malaparte's house built between 1938 and 1942 on the promontory of Punta Masullo, on the eastern side of Capri. A large room suspended on a rock overlooking the sea, four panoramic views, a staircase that widens as it climbs to the roof-terrace, and a screen that looks like a wave. This sophisticated and powerful architecture, the result of a collaboration with Adalberto Libera and builder Ciro Amitrano, summed up the radical idea of a domestic intimacy with the Mediterranean landscape. Villa Malaparte is a place that has continued to live and relive as an icon and backdrop for narratives, as in Jean-Luc Godard's film that set Alberto Moravia's *Contempt* there in 1963. The majolica and wooden frames designed by Alberto Savinio appear in the footage, as well as the roof of the house measured by Brigitte Bardot's footsteps.
This relationship between cinema, architecture, and the Mediterranean landscape recurs cyclically, as happens with the domed house designed by Dante Bini for Michelangelo Antonioni and Monica Vitti in 1969 on the

coast of western Gallura, Sardinia. They are just a few hundred meters from the island of Budelli, where a passionate love was born on the sand of the Spiaggia Rosa a few years earlier, during the filming of *Red Desert* (1964).
For the dome, Bini had devised an ingenious mode of construction: a concrete casting that was inflated through air pressure and then pierced to accommodate the window frames. It was a kind of integrated prefabrication, which was created in one fell swoop by constructive invention; but also, the architectural metaphor of a fulminating passion. The dome (there are actually two, one being a small outbuilding a few meters away) would cease to live with the end of the love between the two, and today, after years of neglect, it is almost a ruin.

And it is hard for me not to recognize a similar idea of domestic intimacy with the changing landscape of the Mediterranean, with its colors, winds, and rocks, when I think of the construction that my mother, Cini Boeri, built for our family in 1967, on the northern tip of the island of La Maddalena. It is a construction that, like Bini's dome, is a bunker. In this case, a truncated lime-cement pyramid, designed to shelter from the winds and the saline of the waves.
In the 1970s, it saw other protagonists of Italian cinema pass through its walls, such as Gianmaria Volonté, who wanted to be buried on the island, or Elio Petri, the director of such unforgettable films as *Investigation of a Citizen Above Suspicion* (1970).
After all, Mediterranean houses are like movies. And, like their cities, they are by nature open to the unpredictability of the flow of life.

Give Peace a Chance (1994)

Promised Lands

I fear the domination of authoritarian forces

Amos Gitai

My grandfather boarded a ship in Odessa bound for Alexandria, and from there, he arrived in Jaffa on a camel. This was in 1905. My grandmother and he belonged to that generation at the beginning of the twentieth century that felt deeply concerned about the great utopias of that era. They had broken ties with their families to come here, especially my grandmother, who came from a prominent family of very orthodox Jews. When my grandmother announced that she was leaving for Palestine, her parents declared a shiv'a: they considered her dead. Not only had she followed the man she loved, but she hadn't waited for a sign from the Messiah to go to Palestine! This judgment troubled her all her life. Later, when my maternal great-grandparents came to the Holy Land to die in Safed, the great center of Kabbalah in Galilee, they visited her but didn't want to enter her house. They met outside, on the doorstep.

I remember that my mother, when I was a child, asked me to accompany her to Safed. She wanted to find her grandfather's grave. But an earthquake had destroyed much of the cemetery. The caretaker discovered a fragment of the tombstone of my family. All these fragments of biography, these pieces of stone, make up the modern history and contemporary reality of Israel.

Israeli identity is also made up of the broken lives of the Palestinians who were displaced and exiled by the Israelis. Some were living in their villages but were declared absent by the authorities because they were not present on a specific date in 1948. So they were displaced, and since then, they have looked at their own history, their own houses, which were taken over by the Israelis. Israeli identity is also the story of North African Jews, who came from Morocco, Tunisia, Algeria, and

Libya, to whom Ben-Gurion had assigned the role of filling the void left by the departure of the Arabs. They have not forgiven the Labor Party for their paternalistic attitude. Israel is constituted by people who, for the most part, have had rather complicated lives and have navigated through infinite labyrinths: those who arrived, driven by a social project, a new socialist, Zionist world, fueled by the desire to realize their ideal; or those who landed, pushed by history, ejected by Europe, with equally challenging journeys. Israel is the culmination of a century of odysseys, layered like temporal archaeological strata.

My father, an architect trained by the Bauhaus, was arrested by the Nazis in 1933, imprisoned, beaten, and finally expelled to Switzerland, from where he later left for Palestine. Coming from Berlin via Basel, and steeped in the European avant-garde, he had to build a new identity. This world was entirely foreign to him; he perceived it as a kind of "west coast of Asia." On my mother's side, the pioneering spirit was driven by the desire to create original social and political institutions—my maternal grandfather was one of the founders of the Hapoalim Workers' Bank and an editor at the newspaper *Hapoel Hatzaïr* ("The Young Worker").

Like everyone born after the creation of the State of Israel, I am, of course, a product of my family's biography. But also something else. Shaul Tchernichovsky says in a very beautiful poem that man is "the imprint of the landscape of his birth." I have not directly experienced being a Jew of the diaspora; I am a citizen of a State, which I hope will be able to extend its democratic principles to all its citizens and maintain the institutions that will always enable it to continue the dialogue. I fear the dominance of authoritarian forces. Israel was a refuge for Jews at a certain time; the question today is what kind of society it will become.

Throughout different eras, there have been very different interpretations of what can be called "Israeli identity." In the 1920s, many of the early pioneers and writers, like Bialik, for example, despite their enthusiasm for founding a new country and a new language, felt like strangers in this land. Many found themselves suddenly transplanted from Central Europe to the heat of the Middle East. The second generation wanted to cut ties with the history of the diaspora and create a new culture, inheriting the history of Palestine as a geographical place; these were the ones called the Canaanites.

Their references were no longer the Judaism of two thousand years of diaspora, but the Hebraism of the time before those two millennia. The history of the pagan tribes that inhabited Palestine even before the Hebrews. This movement welcomed artists like Yitzhak Danziger, a sculptor of German origin who was my teacher, as well as poets like Ratosh. All of them wanted to create a culture radically disconnected from the Jewish experience. The pioneers wanted to show the world that Jews are not just merchants and intellectuals, but can also be farmers and soldiers. Jews transformed their history into secular institutions—having a State, a Supreme Court, etc.—structures that are now threatened by a religious and nationalist wave that disregards the existence of other Israeli citizens of Arab origin and seeks to establish racist values and discrimination against Palestinians.

According to historian and philosopher Gershom Scholem, with the State of Israel, Jews have returned to the stage of history. They are no longer passive subjects pushed around by the winds and currents of world history, discriminated against, burned, massacred; they have taken their destiny into their own hands. But acting isn't utopian. We face contradictions and dilemmas. We commit injustices for which we must be held accountable.

The Israeli–Palestinian conflict occupies a significant place in global attention. From the very beginning, Ben-Gurion had assigned an essential role to cinema. When he was Prime Minister, he even entrusted its management to his cabinet. His reference was Soviet cinema and socialist realism in his approach to managing and controlling the country's image. But he was also the heir of Theodor Herzl, the founder of the Zionist movement. From the outset, this movement made use of imagery. In Palestine, Herzl was accompanied by a photographer and ensured that his handshake with Kaiser Wilhelm II was immortalized. Unfortunately, the photo didn't turn out well. Back in Jaffa, the photographer realized in his lab that the Kaiser was there in the photo, but only Herzl's foot could be seen! So Herzl returned to Jaffa, and they created a photomontage that circulated worldwide: the Kaiser had promised the Holy Land to the Jews. It's no coincidence that Ben-Gurion placed cinema under his cabinet's control.

Images are considered so precious, so important that the filmmaker is regarded as a suspicious person: What will he show? What will people say? The goyim? You shouldn't show this to the goyim . . . One must understand that Israel, in an almost African sense, is a kind of clan, an extended family. In such a social structure, the individual doesn't have the full right to speak, to criticize the tribe. Yet, the medium of cinema requires a critical perspective. All artistic work demands imposing some distance, for a simple optical reason: when you're too close, you can't focus properly, it's blurry. Building a critical distance between oneself and the object being shown sometimes leads to challenging relationships in Israel.

Israel is a modern society and, like many modern societies, it's schizophrenic. Our era forces us to live several lives simultaneously. Encounters are unpredictable. Chance is a fundamental ingredient of our experience. This creates a profound existential crisis that is distinctly Western and specifically Israeli. This is what I wanted to show in *Devarim* (1995), for instance. In this film, Goldman's mother is part of a generation that forged its identity against discrimination, while Goldman no longer has this struggle to face. Like this segment of Israeli society that didn't choose to be born in Israel, Goldman seeks his identity. What does secularism mean? Why should military service continue?

Some people cope through highly materialistic attitudes of excessive consumption, but there isn't a dominant answer as there was for the previous generation. One aspect of modernity is accepting that a life is not necessarily an accomplishment. My films are often juxtapositions of biographies, with memories of the past, sentimental relationships, existential dilemmas, all sorts of fractures. Through this fragmentation, the characters try to build themselves and maintain coherence in a non-coherent context.

My film sets are often meeting places for people from different backgrounds. This was the case in *Ana Arabia* (2013): Israeli and Palestinian actors and actresses came together on the set, a slum in the heart of Tel Aviv. In the face of a kind of disintegration of the original ideology, they are searching for a new sense of existence, a humanistic sense. I believe it's important to talk about modernity, about the lifestyle in Israel. The lives of men and women there aren't different from those in other countries, with their struggles, their conflicts in love and sex. But they unfold in a dramatic local context.
I believe we need to talk about our daily experiences, our inner lives, without exoticism. With *Kadosh* (1999), I wanted to show that Israel is a composite society, and that this country cannot be understood using slogans. The civil society is made up of various groups: religious, mixed Jewish–Arab, etc. It's not homogeneous, and that's what I like. With each film, the puzzle becomes more complex because I try to show different angles. My mother's grandparents and my father's parents, for example, were not that far from the characters in *Kadosh*. When I made this film, I talked a lot with my mother. Her anti-religious attitude was linked to her childhood memories. My parents were always secular, they were proud to be Jews and didn't have any inferiority complex. But they had a strong sense of solidarity tied to suffering. They believed that this long history of persecution had created a bond within this scattered community, a collective commitment that they expressed in modern, non-religious terms. I don't feel any sentimentality. For me, Jewish tradition is first and foremost a great critical school.
During the Yom Kippur War in 1973, I was part of a rescue team. For us, the enemy was death: we had to save people. When our helicopter flew over Syrian territory, I saw villages, jeeps, bases, and that's when the missile hit us and our helicopter crashed. From rescuers, we became victims. It took me twenty-seven years before I could make a fictional film about this experience. I am aware that I am just an individual within this vast mechanism, perhaps a witness, almost in the Hitchcockian sense of the word: that of being a witness to a crime. I won't speak in terms of a mission, but there's something I must convey

through my own perspective. Moreover, Israel is a very touching country. Things are very raw, not hidden, rather exposed. All of this deserves a strong perspective.
From the beginning, memory has played a significant role in my work. Sometimes it serves as a compass, guiding the way we envision the future. You can't be eternally content to judge things based on the present; sometimes you have to look back.
When I was a child, my mother always left two train tickets on the shelf above the breakfast table. On these two tickets, it said "Haifa–Beirut." My parents had spent their honeymoon in Baalbek, Lebanon, in the 1930s, but now the borders were closed. I asked her, "Why do you take out these tickets? Lebanon is an enemy country." I still think about how she replied: "It was possible before, and maybe it will be possible again one day." These sealed borders, this excess of nationalism, and everything that follows aren't inevitable.
When Yitzhak Rabin was assassinated on November 4, 1995, I felt that a page of history had been turned. In this context, the problem for the artist, the filmmaker, is figuring out what to do when living near a volcano. You have to offer a perspective. And that's not easy. So, a few years ago, we decided to make *Rabin, the Last Day* (2015), as a kind of gesture of memory. With the very hope that resurrecting memory can make things change.
In Israel, we are confronted with political reality: today, there is a lack of a figure who would have the courage, I'd even say the optimism, despite everything happening in the Middle East, to move forward, to reach out, to create a dialogue. This absence of a visionary figure is dramatic. In this context, the film, the play, and the exhibitions I dedicated to Rabin's assassination become a civic act.
When I made *Field Diary*, before and during the Lebanon War of 1982, I had the same feeling: the points of conflict kept expanding due to the policies implemented by the Israeli government. The current situation is a complete deadlock. The Israeli government in power is very reactionary. It intervenes in all areas, including justice, culture, and education, to limit freedom of expression and circulate racist rhet-

oric. In the absence of political solutions to resolve the issue of occupation, men and women are rising and acting in the name of their civic conscience. That's what I wanted to show in *West of the Jordan River* (2017), a tribute to the courage of these people who feel disappointed, like me, and compelled to act personally.
The struggle these associations lead is not easy. It generates antagonism, even hatred. They are often mistreated, and yet they remain convinced of the need to reach out, in good faith, to the Palestinians who have been under occupation for fifty years. That is, two-thirds of the existence of this country, Israel. These associations raise ethical and moral questions among the public. They are living proof that there are Israelis sincerely seeking reconciliation and that the country doesn't belong solely to the politicians currently in power.

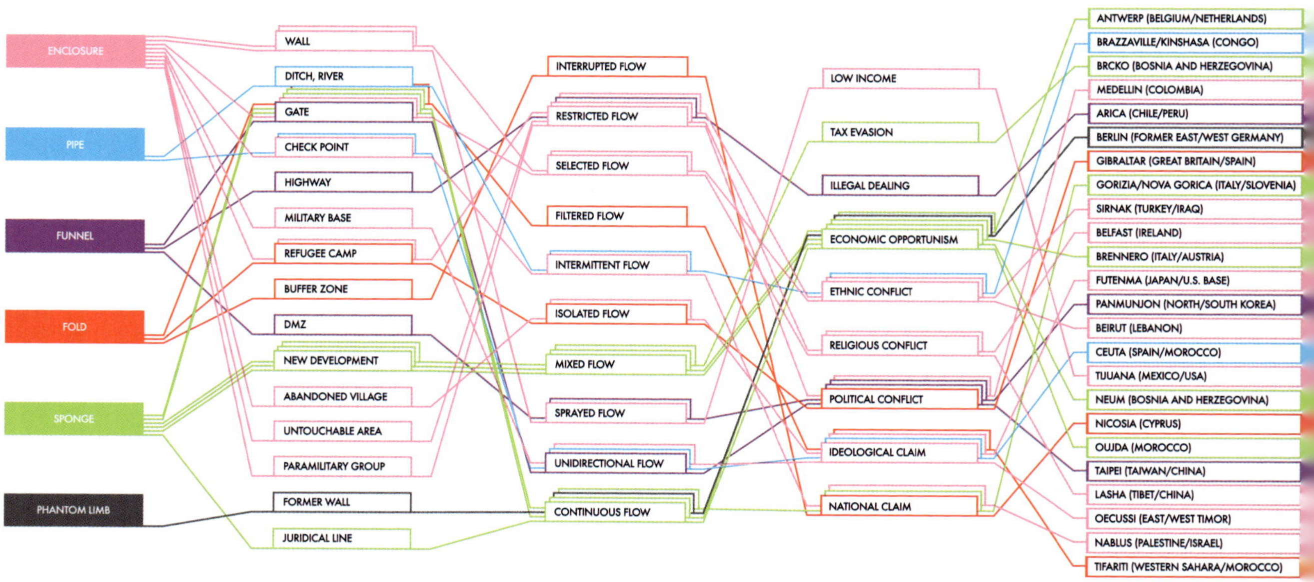

Multiplicity with Berlage Institute Rotterdam for *Domus* no. 872, *The matrix of borders*, drawn from the research *Border Device(s)*, 2003

Border Device(s)

The road map

Stefano Boeri

Border Device(s) was the title of the research for the 2003 *Territories* exhibition at Kunst-Werke Berlin and the 50th Venice Biennale.
Back then, it seemed to us that the processes of globalization had paradoxically generated its opposite: a proliferation of borders, checkpoints, security systems, protected areas, and buffer zones. This phenomenon could and can still be observed both at the level of what strictly surrounds us and on a global scale.
Border Device(s) was an investigation that revealed how, looking at global flows (of people, goods, and ideas) and territorial restrictions in parallel, it is always possible to unveil how individual and collective identities are defined in all their complexity in the act of crossing the borders imposed by geopolitics.

More generally, *Border Device(s)* allowed us to understand how borders, in geopolitical terms, are always "devices," in the sense indicated by Mi-

Multiplicity, Map highlighting the different travel times of the Israeli and Palestinian taxi drivers, from *The Road Map*, 2003

Multiplicity, Frames of the Israeli and Palestinian taxi drivers' journeys, from *The Road Map*, 2003

chel Foucault and specified by Gilles Deleuze. Indeed, states and geopolitical borders are the intentional outcome of active social and cultural processes, behind which stand established power relations. And borders, in their form and nature, reflect these power relations.

For this reason, we began to construct a kind of taxonomy of borders, or rather their original matrices.

These matrices started from the study of twenty-four cases of boundary lines in the world.

Indeed, the research on border devices stemmed from a series of field investigations, as was usual for Multiplicity.

In those years, special attention was dedicated to the territories of Israel and Palestine, which appeared to us then, as they do today, to be a veritable laboratory, a region where, in just a few hectares, an incredible variety of borders, fences, checkpoints, and monitored corridors are concentrated.

And the first of these investigations, conducted by Salvatore Porcaro, Sandi Hilal and Alessandro Petti, was precisely in the West Bank, in the area of the so-called "occupied territories."

The Road Map installation, with the videos and maps of the two journeys, was presented at Kunstwerke Berlin in 2003 accompanied by the following text:

> "On January 13 and 14, 2003, we attempted to measure the density of border checkpoints in the areas surrounding Jerusalem using our EU passports.

On January 13, specifically, we traveled along Highway 60 with a person holding an Israeli passport, from the Kiryat Arba settlement to the Kedumim settlement.
The following day, we traveled with a person holding a Palestinian passport from the city of Hebron to the city of Nablus.
Both routes started and ended at the same latitude: in some points, they overlapped. However, their travel times were significantly different.
To travel between the two latitudes, the Israeli traveler took approximately one hour, while the Palestinian traveler took five and a half hours.

At that time, the territories of the West Bank were divided into three different zones:
Zone A, under the military and administrative control of the Palestinian Authority, included most Palestinian cities.
Zone B was under Israeli military control but under the administrative control of the Palestinian Authority. It primarily included Palestinian villages.
Zone C, under Israeli military and administrative control, comprised most Israeli settlements.

This division had created a patchwork territory where the three zones alternated without apparent logic.

The different travel times of the two routes were due to the fact that Israeli travelers moving from one settlement to another—from one Zone C to another Zone C—could use the so-called 'bypass roads': highways, often in tunnels or elevated roads that connected the settlements by circumventing Palestinian villages.
On the other side, Palestinian travelers moving from one city to another in Zone A had to pass through Zones B or C, which were under Israeli military control, crossing a number of permanent and temporary checkpoints—or trying to avoid them.
The checkpoints, located along the 'Green Line' that runs between Israel and the West Bank as well as on the edges of East Jerusalem, could not be crossed by those with a 'travel document' issued by the Palestinian Authority without a special permit issued by the Israeli government. Other checkpoints were activated and removed daily according to Israeli government's security guidelines.

In summary, the field investigation not only revealed a very intricate spectrum of border devices that were more or less visible, more or less formalized and legally legitimate, but above all, it confirmed how the border always acts as a device for encoding and confirming the identity of those who cross it, and thus also as a selective device that produces inequalities, as in the case of the research conducted in the West Bank."

At the conclusion of the field investigations, extended to 23 case studies, we began drafting an initial list of "border devices," which would later be published on the cover of *Domus* issue no. 872 in 2004.
The six matrices of border devices were:
- Funnel borders, which channel a flow in one direction;
- Pipe borders, which channel a flow but subject it to unilateral or bilateral control;
- Fold borders, which create an interstitial space whose characteristics do not belong to either of the two realities separated by the border line;
- Sponge borders, which attract flows of all kinds that settle along the border line, thickening it;
- "Phantom limb" borders, which continue to act even if they have physically disappeared, resulting in the collective memory regenerating the border line;
- Enclosure borders, which segregate a community of individuals and a system of activities within a perimeter, whose control is often unilateral.

In a world torn apart by wars and conflicts, in a geopolitical landscape where emerging empires and declining empires confront each other, the study of border devices remains an essential task for deciphering the identities and purposes of the forces at play.

Unheimliche
Uncanny territories
Stefano Boeri

Translating concepts, ideas, and paradigms from distant realms of knowledge into architecture is a useful yet risky exercise. As previously mentioned, the work of an architect inherently involves a dual movement: the first, which is inclusive, demands the assimilation of suggestions, ideas, and concepts from fields different from our own. The second, concurrent with the first, is a movement that shifts through the myriad gathered ideas, selecting them in a manner that nourishes a single project capable of gradually acquiring a precise form and spatiality.
To design means to be open to the world and, simultaneously, to equip oneself with the necessary ruthlessness that compels us to exclude the majority of suggestions collected in favor of a singular formal configuration, endowed with an increasingly defined and precise dimension and gravity.

I believe that this simultaneous dual movement explains how there is an inherent dose of schizophrenia in architects. Moreover, I have never believed in projects born from lengthy analyses or in analytical studies that arise directly from a simple design idea. Or, better said, I have never believed in the actual possibility of rigidly placing the inclusion of a world of possibilities and the selection within a chronological sequence, within a before and after, of a single, unique, formal solution.
But there's more. In truth, the irrepressible curiosity for the world and the ability to arrive, in solitude, at a single way of envisioning the future of a space are the most effective means for triggering the sudden synapses between the enrichment of knowledge and the construction of that sort of "conceptual hologram" (a term I borrow from conversations with Renzo Piano contained in *Being Renzo Piano*, a special issue of *Abitare* no. 497 dedicated to him) that lies at the origin of an architectural project.

opposite page
Stefano Boeri Architetti, *Radura*, installation inside the Bramante courtyard at Università degli Studi, Milan, Italy, 2016

That being said, it is undeniable that some architects are more adept than others at translating and utilizing concepts that come from other worlds and realms of knowledge.

Some of my insights stem from the intense study of Michel Foucault, a philosopher, historian, and anthropologist who lived in France between 1926 and 1984. I owe my passion for Foucault—as well as the suggestion of a number of foundational readings for my work as an urban planner and architect—to my association with Bernardo Secchi, my first mentor. In the late seventies, Secchi was deeply immersed in Foucault's texts; *The Archaeology of Knowledge* (1969) and *The Order of Things: An Archaeology of the Human Sciences* (1966) held for his students a significance akin to those foundational texts in architecture and urban planning. We weren't concerned with translating concepts of philosophical origin clumsily into architectural terminology; rather, we aimed to let "chemical reactions" occur within our reflections and practices.
Many years later, while grappling with a challenging transition in my professional life, I found myself drawing on the effects of the quiet labor of one of these concepts/enzymes: that which links the issue of madness to a dimension of internality.

In a dialogue that took place in 1971 in Eindhoven, Michel Foucault confronted philosopher and linguist Noam Chomsky about the definition of the concept of "human nature" (*The Chomsky–Foucault Debate: On Human Nature*). The positions of these two giants of thought and their implications in twentieth-century politics are far apart.
While Chomsky insists on the Enlightenment capacity of reason to control human nature, calling into question the technologies of rationality, Foucault's intervention is disorienting: in French (in a place where only English or Dutch are spoken), he declares how human nature should rather be approached as madness, the uncontrollable emergence of a disruption of reason itself, something that unhinges its order of discourse from within. According to Foucault, madness does not originate from an external factor; it is not a disease or a contamination. Rather, madness is

Frame from *The Chomsky–Foucault Debate on Human Nature*, Eindhoven University of Technology, October 22, 1971

a state of mind that arises within human nature, in its innermost sphere. It is a sudden, often angry, unpredictable, and uncontrolled emergence from within the very codes of reason.

A few years ago, when I was involved in the reconstruction projects in the areas of Central Italy hit by the 2016 earthquake, I was reminded of this conception of human nature and the analogy Foucault establishes with madness.
Our work focused particularly on Amatrice—whose historic center had totally been destroyed by the earthquake and where 299 people lost their lives—and Norcia.
In Amatrice, between November 2016 and June 2017, through public fundraising, we helped to rebuild the school canteen and eight of the restaurants demolished by the earthquake. In Norcia, a few months later—following the collapse of churches, buildings, and community gathering places due to seismic tremors—we were asked by the municipality and the Civil Defense to create a temporary hub to replace the destroyed public and collective spaces to house inhabitants in case of subsequent disasters and emergencies.

Why, in that dramatic context, should we rethink the analogy between human madness and nature? Why associate it with the catastrophic event of an earthquake?

Stefano Boeri Architetti, Emergency wooden settlement "Il Polo del Gusto,"
built few months after the earthquake in Amatrice, 2017

Like madness, an earthquake often manifests as the sudden betrayal of a rational and habitual order, destroying centuries of history and decades of individual memories in a matter of seconds. It is a particularly disturbing event because, as Augusto Placanica, author of *Il filosofo e la catastrofe* (The Philosopher and the Catastrophe; 1985), reminds us, unlike other natural disasters, it arises from the ground we tread, from the very foundation of our lives—something that in psychoanalysis, particularly in Sigmund Freud's thinking, comes close to the concept of the *Unheimliche*, a term for a phenomenon that is both familiar and disturbing.

An earthquake is the manifestation of an unpredictable event that emerges from the intimacy of a place of our everyday lives; it arises from that very soil that we are used to considering a habitual, friendly, passive host of our daily life. It is a betrayal that not only invokes the image of a nature that "goes mad," but also—in analogy with the notion of madness—helps us understand the impacts on the subsequent life choices of those affected.

I believe there are two prevailing reactions. One is to experience this trauma as an irreversible discontinuity, leading to the decision to leave forever the place that has betrayed you. The biographies of those displaced by the endless series of earthquakes that have occurred on Italian soil testify to a cleanly truncated relationship, one no longer recovered. Often those who leave never return.

However, there is also another way of reacting: a more or less conscious way that pushes us to remove the trauma. The possibility of dealing with the place that betrayed us can be accepted only by removing the discontinuity, only if one thinks about the possibility of rebuilding the space and places erased by the earthquake "as it was and where it was." The dream of a reconstruction that somehow removes the traumatic event is nothing but one of human reactions to the madness of an unpredictable nature, manifesting itself within friendly territory.

When we found ourselves working for Amatrice, we were immediately confronted with those who had developed these two opposite reactions but shared a common trait: the difficulty of coming to terms with the present and the attempt to replace it with the possibility of a return to the past. Talking with the relatives of the victims, we could feel, almost physically, the cry for help in imagining the possibility of removing that unforeseen and insane disturbance that, coming from the ground they trod, from the territory they knew best, had transfigured their lives. For that reason, too, working in those areas was and still is a very strong and indelible experience, from which we have so much to learn.

In the same way, the pandemic has compelled us to rethink the concept of nature as something intimately inherent within us and, at the same time, extremely powerful and entirely uncontrollable.

But beyond that of "nature," perhaps it is time to reconsider and reinterpret the concept of "technology" as well.
In his work *Metamorphoses* (2021), Emanuele Coccia tells us how technology—meant as metamorphosis made possible through a highly technical process—is a dimension that belongs to nature. It makes no sense, he argues, to oppose technology as a sphere of knowledge generated by rationality and culture to a wild nature. The presence of sophisticated technology even in natural processes, Coccia continues, is evidenced by the example of chlorophyll synthesis: something we have not yet been able to artificially replicate, and through which forests, trees, and woods enable all other living beings on the planet to survive by producing oxygen and absorbing the carbon dioxide that our species continues to produce at increasingly accelerated rates.
On the other hand, we are accustomed to exclusively associating the concept of nature with the plant world and non-domestic animal species: a reality that we tend to keep separate from the realm of the human sphere and which holds, within it, a logic that appears indecipherable to us.

As paradoxical as it may seem, I often find myself thinking that the most powerful and unpredictable natural phenomena are not so much those related to the life rhythms of the plant world and wildlife, but rather—and this is not meant to be provocative—to the disturbances and energies that accompany urban social conflicts, unleashing sudden and uncontrollable convulsions. These conflicts, which always constitute a form of social interaction inherent to the urban and metropolitan condition, are likely to undergo a significant acceleration in the coming months and years.

The vast scale of migratory flows resulting from the (so far unstoppable) curve of global warming will render entire regions of the planet uninhabitable in the coming decades. Due to the progressive desertification of the southern hemisphere of the planet, hundreds of millions of climate refugees will move toward Australia, Europe, and North America, resulting in a dimensional and social explosion of those informal settlements

Stefano Boeri Architetti, House of the Sea, La Maddalena, Sardinia, Italy, 2009

(slums, shantytowns, favelas . . .) that already house more than 30% of the world's urban population today.

Slums are now a true city within the city and effectively represent the only urban form capable of promptly accommodating waves of migratory flows mainly from the poorest regions of the planet. In the absence of adequate redistributive policies and social welfare, the explosion of informal settlements will lead to a multiplication of areas of absolute poverty and conflict among urban populations in the world's metropolises, which will once again be revealed as great vibrant collectors of the most disparate human lives. This is an unstoppable phenomenon that we studied between 2012 and 2014 through field research in the favelas of São Paulo, Brazil, coordinated by Lorenza Baroncelli (published in 2012 in the supplement of *Domus* no. 963, *São Paulo Calling*).

When we talk about biometropolises, biocities, we must also consider the scope of naturalness, of ungovernable vitality, of the potential "madness" of social conflicts. We must think of the large urban spaces pulsating and innervated by the tensions of social life, which, as much as they may be guided by rational plans and wise public policies by local governance, will be traversed by profound transformations that will change their cultural and demographic composition.
The truth is that the risk of an exacerbation of metropolitan social conflict, a widespread explosion of urban revolts, is a concrete possibility in the future of our cities. Therefore, we should ask ourselves how to anticipate this risk, reducing its most dramatic and unforeseen effects. But to do this, we would need a new paradigm of urban life, one capable of conceiving the idea of an urbanity interconnected with natural phenomena and their vital characteristics.
In cities, in homes, in our bodies, whether we like it or not, we already host nature, because we *are* nature.

opposite page
São Paulo Calling Manifesto, curated by Stefano Boeri and Lorenza Baroncelli, 2012

São Paulo Calling Manifesto

1
Favelas are metropolises
3 million people live in the favelas of Sao Paulo. 8 million live in the slums of Mumbai. 2.5 million in the shantytowns of Nairobi. An informal settlement is not an extraneous alien superfetation, but an important and constituent part of the contemporary city.

2
Favelas are fast
An informal city grows faster than the public administration is able to plan its development.

3
Favelas are necessary
For thousands of migrants and peasants, informal settlements are the first access to urban life. They are the physical embodiment of an unstoppable flow of urbanisation that moves millions of the planet's inhabitants per year from the countryside to the city.

4
Favelas are many small towns
Often distant from the city centre (but sometimes wedged into it) favelas are isolated, autonomous, distinct systems that turn their urban unit into many small "towns".

5
Favelas are never the same
Each favela has its own character, language, activities, music, rituals and aspirations.
Each functions according to its own organisation logics and identity.

5
Favelas are dynamic urban areas of production and commerce
The need to survive, combined with the absence of restrictions and regulations, encourages the development of small crafts businesses and civic services that substitute public welfare agencies. This makes for a molecular market of micro-produced goods.

7
Favelas represent a spontaneous model of a "knowledge economy"
In the favelas you can live cheaply and decide to learn something. Every idea can become a trade, and creativity produces economy.

8
Favelas represent a new model of very dense molecular urbanisation and socialisation
Informal settlements have a unique physical structure, composed of thousands of small constructions all crammed together: a compact, minute and intimate structure where every nook and cranny is full of life.
Intimacy here means that everyone knows about everyone else's life: intimacy with one's neighbours for better or for worse.

9
Favelas are an ideal place for legal and illegal forms of self-organisation
Favelas host, and often nurture, legal and illegal forms of selforganisation: religious associations, trade groups, and criminal organisations that supply the illegal drug markets. The degree and nature of self-organisation can increase the favelas' degree of protection from and closure toward the outside world.

10
Favelas are ever changing
Favelas are under constant transformation, evolving steadily. They change and grow, satisfying the mutating needs of the individuals and families who inhabit them.
Their development is incremental, configured as it is by the life story of every migrant, every family and every community living there.

11
Favelas are viral cities
Favelas are ecological cities that never change the landscape irreversibly. They are also viral, seeping into and occupying every free crack, turning the "third landscape" into a place of humanorganic nature. All space is invaded; there are no gaps where the city slows down and breathes.

Therefore, favelas are an essential part of the contemporary city.

Informal settlements are not temporary. They are part and parcel of a city that already exists. Architecture, social networks and economic activities are irretrievably entangled, like the roots and branches of a forest. Improving them does not mean thinking of a new city model, but helping a branch to grow so that the others grow too.

The above manifesto was written by Stefano Boeri and Urbz, with contributions by the São Paulo Secretaria Municipal de Habitaçao and the researchers involved in São Paulo Calling

House (1980). Palestinian workers in a quarry near Hebron

House Stories

Microcosm and metaphor

Amos Gitai

The screenplay is always a simulation. Writing a screenplay, to use an architectural metaphor, is a kind of scaffolding or sketch. Using a medium that is not very expensive—paper—the screenplay must simulate the idea of the film, but it should not be executed, and I emphasize the verb "executed" in all its meanings. Cinema that simply executes a concept or a text is limited. It's the process of interpretation that interests me: you have an idea, and that's the starting point. Jeanne Moreau once told me, when she agreed to work with me, "Amos, I only work on films when I think I will learn something I didn't already know." Placing questions in space triggers reflection. For *The War of the Sons of Light Against the Sons of Darkness* (2009), the show created at the Avignon Festival based on Flavius Josephus's text *The Jewish War*, Jeanne surrounded herself with books on the Roman Empire, the beginnings of anti-Semitism, etc. That is to say, the project is always an opportunity to learn more. Often, the camera, this fetish, provides me with a pretext to be present. If I hadn't had a camera with me, I wouldn't have had the opportunity to take a flight with Yitzhak Rabin when he went to negotiate the peace agreement with the Palestinians in Cairo and Washington. It's only this fetish tool, this little object, that legitimized my presence and proved that the event actually took place. The camera becomes the chronicler of our time; in this sense, it is the quintessential modern fetish.

My first film, *House* (1980), is about a house in West Jerusalem that belonged to a Palestinian family of doctors, the Dajanis, until 1948. The film traces the succession of its owners and residents. After the Deir Yassin massacre during the 1948 war, the Dajani family left their home, and the Israeli government housed Algerian Jewish immigrants, the Toboul family, there. After the 1967 war, the borders shifted and Jerusalem was unified. This house ended up in the city center, in a neighborhood called The German Colony, next to Talbiya, where prominent Palestinian families like Edward Said's used to live. After the Dajani family left in 1948, the Toboul s also moved out when in 1967 a renowned Israeli economist, Professor Haim Barkai, managed to relocate them to public housing in Katamon, on the outskirts of Jerusalem. Now, he wants to transform this one-story house into a three-story villa. To do so, he has to bring stones from a quarry near Yatta, south of the West Bank, and Palestinian workers from refugee camps around Hebron. This house is therefore the subject of this documentary, which offers a series of biographical fragments. It's a kind of microcosm, a metaphor for Jerusalem, with its human archaeological layers.

Initially, my idea was to make a film about an industrial machine to which people of different origins would be connected. The routine aspect of working on a machine would have allowed me to evoke a series of biographies: Jews, Arabs, Sephardim, Ashkenazim, religious, secular, etc. But when I actually started working on it, I told myself that I had still been trained as an architect and that I would rather film a house. We found several houses, and we were lucky—not just a matter of intellect or will—to come across this one, whose history included all these contradictions. The film thus begins in the stone quarry: you first see the materials, which will then be transported to the house. Then you meet one of the main protagonists, who works as a stonemason on the construction site. Next comes the encounter with the economist who has just bought this house and gives us a long Milton Friedman-style speech on the market economy. Then we return to the worker cutting stones with his grinder. This is a way, through editing, to cut the economist off mid-speech . . . The film doesn't use voice-over narration. It's a series of juxtaposed fragments. We give each person space to present their point of view, to tell the story of this house, and the conflict is embedded in this microcosm: it's constructed alongside the house itself.

Question *Are you ashamed of being a mason?*

Stonecutter On the contrary. I'm proud to earn my living by the sweat of my brow. I don't steal, and I don't kill to earn my bread. I'm proud to earn my bread.

Question *So why don't you want me to film you?*

Stonecutter What will people say?

Question *They'll see you in work clothes? But working is an honor!*

Stonecutter Some understand, and others think I'm a vagabond.

Question *Who are they?*

Stonecutter Idiots? There are plenty of them.

Question *Where are you from?*

Stonecutter From Walaja.

Question *Walaja? Where's that?*

Stonecutter Our village is occupied. The Jews took it in '48.

Question *Where is it?*

Stonecutter We rebuilt it ourselves. We call it New Walaja, it's near Beit Jala.

Question *Where did you live before? Where was the old village?*

Stonecutter Walaja was next to Battir, in the Jerusalem district.

Question *Was it occupied in '48?*

Stonecutter They took it in '48. They only left us a small plot of land. We lived there from 1950 onward.

Question *Was your old house destroyed?*

Stonecutter Completely razed, by bulldozers. All of it, just to make hatred grow in our hearts.

Question *Do you feel hatred?*

Stonecutter Of course! When I lose my house, my brother, and my son, I feel hatred. You should know that.

Question *So, you hate them?*

Stonecutter I hate them as they hate me. That's the truth.

Question *So what are you doing here?*

Stonecutter I'm working. We have no choice. We're prisoners of Israel. We have to earn our living by working.

Question *Do you know who you're building for?*

Stonecutter I know that this house was originally an Arab house.

Question *Who was the owner?*

Stonecutter A man from the Dajani family.

Question *How does it feel to rebuild it for someone other than the Dajanis?*

Stonecutter It breaks my heart.

Question *Do you know the neighborhood?*

Stonecutter I don't know anything before 1948. I didn't know this region. Our road led to the Old City of Jerusalem and to Beit Safafa, up to the station.

Question *Did anyone tell you about the neighborhood?*

Stonecutter I was told that it was once an Arab neighborhood. Today, its inhabitants are Jews.

Question *What time do you come to work?*

Stonecutter Personally, I have a lot of work this week because of this arch that needs to be finished. I arrive at the construction site at 6 a.m. I go home at 10 p.m.

Question *How much do you earn?*

Stonecutter 550 liras per day. Eight hours of work for 550 liras. Overtime counts for an hour and a half.

Question *Let's go back to our first topic. You say you hate them as much as they hate you. That's still a very harsh word.*

Stonecutter It is harsh. But when someone hurts you, it's hard to forget. We're not like Jesus, who says, "If someone slaps you on the right cheek, turn the other cheek to them also." Our religion says, "An eye for an eye, a tooth for a tooth." So when I see that they destroyed my house, that the bulldozers razed everything, that not a stone remains, and that my village is unrecognizable, it's obvious that I feel hatred.

Question ***And you're rebuilding this house!***

Stonecutter We're rebuilding the house, but on the remains of the Arab house.

Question ***The remains of the Arab house . . .***

Stonecutter But if 36 Arab states haven't managed to defeat Israel, what can our words do against Israel? The wind carries them away. I can't tell you anything more. We have the same God. It will always be according to His will. There's nothing else.

The great advantage of documentary cinema over fiction is the ability to dig deeper. You can return to the same site several times, even after a quarter-century, and this series of human fragments will tell the story of this land over a long period. This film, *House*, is the first in a trilogy made over twenty-five years, from 1980 to 2005. In fiction, you can age the characters with makeup and changes in hairstyle, but here, it's the evolution of our interviewees' discourse over time that's interesting. I believe that the stonemason's ability to describe his story poetically is one of the reasons the film was censored in 1980. In the film, he expresses himself much more richly and subtly than the economist, who was Governor of the Bank of Israel and whose name appears on the banknotes. The fact that language is used in a far more elaborate way by the Palestinian stonemason undermines, in a covert and subversive way, our perception of ourselves, the Israelis, as a sophisticated nation with high culture, a great history, and fine literature. Yet, there are Israelis who believe that Palestinians are "primitive and unable to express themselves." This stonemason contrasts the teachings of Jesus, "turn the other cheek," with "an eye for an eye, a tooth for a tooth," as two opposing views of memory in a much more poetic, and even more threatening, manner for a regime that seeks a simplistic, ethnocentric perception of history. We are not alone, others exist, and cinema can help us realize this. There is no peace if the other doesn't exist. Peace is not a unilateral matter. You must recognize the other, engage in dialogue with them. In cinema, this means depicting them in a non-caricatured way, giving them the time to express themselves and move in space. The body's choreography, the beauty of the worker's gestures, also effectively and necessarily challenge racist assumptions. By saying this, I'm not just referring to the Israeli–Palestinian conflict. Europe is also concerned with the issue of depicting the other, with migrants. The current wave of immigration to Europe is the product of wars largely initiated by Europe, the Americans, and, in general, by foreign powers.

My films touch on a raw nerve. So they hurt and lead to questions. This is my approach: to ask questions. The central question of Israeli–Palestinian relations is that of the Palestinians' attachment to their land. Millions of Palestinians live in refugee camps. This is a time bomb if we, the Israelis, do not manage to address this issue. The question of the right of return is even more complicated than those of Jerusalem and borders. It is the fundamental question. The Yom Kippur War was a battle between the Egyptian and Syrian armies on one side and the Israeli army on the other. But the Israeli–Palestinian conflict is a different matter because this land also belongs to the Palestinians. It's their home, too, their homeland. Confusing these two conflicts will only prolong conflicts in the Middle East. But they must be separated.
The Israeli–Palestinian conflict mobilizes the most media outlets on the planet—back to my discipline. I believe that people in other countries, in Africa, in Asia, also need us to talk about their destinies. But global media want to talk about this Israe-

li–Palestinian series, even though it's not the deadliest conflict in the world if you stick to the numbers. And since it touches on many layers of twentieth-century history and memory—the fate of the Jews—it's associated with several secondary issues that are not directly related to it. How can cinema address the burning issues that need our attention while respecting everyone? This conflict is at the center of relations between the West and the East, between the Judeo–Christian world and the world of Islam. The very territory of Israel connects Europe and Africa, Europe and Asia. In this explosive context, what can a small filmmaker who is making a film about a house in Jerusalem do?

Often, the key moments of my biography have coincided with significant events in Israel's history: the Yom Kippur War in 1973 and this film, my first real film, marked a change in power in the country. In 1977, the Labor Party lost the elections for the first time, and the right appointed a new Director General of Television, Yosef "Tommy" Lapid. He immediately asked me to cut certain passages, like the one you just read. So I found myself facing a dilemma: Should I accept to self-censor my film, consider censorship as just an episode in my life, and remain an architect, or should I fight to defend the film? As Robert Frost's poem says: "I took the road less traveled by," which put me in direct collision with my dear compatriots. It was painful and difficult.

When making a film, you have to be open, welcome all perspectives, and embrace contradictions without trying to indoctrinate, even for a "good cause." You have to show things. *House* juxtaposes fragments of biographies as they are—we're in 1980, and there's still a certain Israeli naivety in believing that if you don't talk about Palestinian memory, it won't exist. But you must talk about memory. It's a powerful agent of change, even if the work of memory doesn't have a direct impact, even if the filmmaker, the writer, and the painter can't replace politicians. In the 1930s, Guernica wasn't just a beautiful painting. It was a civic gesture by an artist, Picasso, who was shocked by the Luftwaffe's bombing of that Basque village and decided to paint it. Today, we admire the beauty of the work, but we must not forget that Picasso had forbidden it to be shown in Spain as long as Franco was alive. This means that artists have ways of imposing sanctions. A few years ago, a political coincidence wanted the new Spanish Prime Minister, a left-wing elected official, to decide to bury Franco's body elsewhere than in his kitschy mausoleum. This is the result of the actions of those who fought for generations against Spanish fascism. Memory is not innocent.

In the second part of the trilogy, *A House in Jerusalem* (1998), I decided to keep the same protagonists but to expand the field horizontally and vertically, starting from this nucleus that is the house, to observe the attachment of Israelis, Jews, Palestinians, and Muslims to this city of Jerusalem. In the final part, *News from Home, News from House* (2005), I expanded the field even further. I decided to show the Palestinian diaspora, meaning that the fragmentation of this conflict led to the fragmentation of the biographies of all those involved. I went to Amman, Jordan, to film the Dajani family, particularly the aunt, an exceptional woman. And then I returned to see the stonemason already mentioned.

In 2005, twenty-five years after the first film, I went back to film the house and met one of its residents, Claire, a charming woman who tells us her story. She was born in Istanbul. She says to me:

Claire You want me to talk about this doctor who was unhappy to see his house, the house of his childhood, occupied by others and which has now passed to another state. We must call it what it is. And I think I would have liked him to ring my doorbell and say to me: "Listen . . . ," and I would have said to him: "I'm sorry, but I didn't make history." I don't want to undo it either, that's the main thing. I didn't make it, but I don't want to undo it. I would maybe like to correct it. That said, when I go to Turkey, I cry because I go to see the house where I was born, and I say to myself that I can't even . . . It's over for everyone. For me, it's not history . . . Well, it is a bit of history anyway because we were a minority, and maybe if we hadn't been a minority, we wouldn't have left so easily? I don't know. It's less tragic than for this doctor; it's obviously less tragic. But I'm not responsible for history because it's like saying: "The Arabs aren't responsible for the Holocaust . . ." It's true, but history happened that way. I don't know if it could have happened differently; I don't know. But I would be happy if we got to know each other.

The idea of *House* was to juxtapose biographical fragments of different people to respect their paths. Claire may be an intelligent, pleasant woman, but she finds herself in an impossible situation. There is a material aspect of existence that is inevitable, even tragic: even lovely, intelligent, and cultured people are prisoners of this situation of being occupiers if Israel cannot find a modus vivendi. These moderate, non-racist people who don't adhere to the current ideology are in full contradiction. To show you the power of a documentary film that respects these contradictions and shares this reflection with you, spectators, it took me time. Time is essential in all artistic fields—cinema, theater, even literature. Because the compression of time achieved by "efficient" montage eliminates the possibility for spectators to think while watching. But if we're given a space for reflection, if we're able not to behave as cinema consumers but as interpreters, it invites us to engage, to form our opinion while watching. You can agree with a certain point of view or, on the contrary, oppose it, but keeping in mind the need to respect each other gives you a more complete idea of the different positions.

It's not just a question of property but of memory and attachment to the same lands, which continues to concern me, and which I addressed in a short film, *A Letter to a Friend in Gaza* (2018), in tribute to Albert Camus' *Letters to a German Friend*, written in 1943. This issue continues to worry me.

I don't believe much in neutrality or in the idea of making "balanced" work, as television claims. As soon as you propose a frame, a simple frame to define reality, you've made a decision. Because you also decide what will be excluded from the frame. It's a series of deliberate steps. Cinema expresses a point of view. There is nothing objective, by definition. Shows and reports are also subjective gestures, whether they come from Israeli, Palestinian, American, French television, etc. The question I always ask is this: How can cinema fit into this complex reality? Because the Middle East is bombarded with images from all sorts of media. What strategy can a filmmaker have not to adhere to these often simplistic and Manichean representations?
First, there's a question of rhythm: not speeding up but offering temporal blocks, long takes, in which contradictions are embedded within the shot itself, without being compressed. In this way, you respect the temporality of an event, and this rhythm allows for reflection during the screening. You don't have to consume the image. It's a commitment made to the spectators.
Another possible strategy is to compose trilogies. With my trilogy on Israeli cities—*Devarim* (1995) about Tel Aviv, *Yom Yom* (1998) about Haifa, and *Kadosh* (1999) about Jerusalem—I suggest that this country doesn't have a single image but is composite. *House* (1980, 1998, 2005) and *Wadi* (1981, 1991,

2001), which tells a love story between a Jewish woman, Miriam, and her Palestinian friend, Iskander, in Haifa, my hometown, are two documentary trilogies. *Field Diary* dates back to 1982. The idea was that the film titles reflect Israeli–Palestinian relations. *House*, in Hebrew *Bait* (the house), *Wadi*, an Arabic word meaning "valley," and *Field Diary*, in Hebrew *Yoman sade*: the conflict is about the territory, the house, the valley, the fields. These three films form a trilogy in themselves, but *House* and *Wadi* also gave birth to children and grandchildren, with a gap of ten and twenty-five years. A quarter-century is a considerable period that allows for the description of a whole series of human relationships, drawing a way of observing details, speeches, biographies, and juxtapositions of biographical fragments.

House (1980)

following pages
Stage version of *House*, Théâtre national de la Colline, Paris, France, 2023

Vertical Forest

Barons in the trees

Stefano Boeri

The Baron in the Trees (1957), a well-known novel by Italo Calvino published in 1957, is one of the three texts that the writer brought together in 1960 in the trilogy called *Our Ancestors*.
I have several versions and editions of it, including the one found in Mondadori's Meridiani collection, which hosts Calvino's complete works.
Set in 1767, *The Baron in the Trees* tells the story of a young twelve-year-old nobleman, narrated by the voice of his brother Biagio. The young baron, Cosimo Piovasco di Rondò (Rondò is a small village in the hinterland of the Ligurian Riviera—I will explain later why this detail is important to me), decides, after a quarrel with his very boring father, to abandon not only his home, not only his family, not only his friends, but the entire community and its familiar places. Cosimo decides to spend the rest of his life in the trees—on the oaks, cork oaks, holm oaks, among the chestnuts, which are the botanical world of this beautiful part of the Italian and Ligurian territory. Living in the trees, among the branches, Cosimo leads a full and adventurous life: he meets extraordinary characters like the bandit Gian de Brughi, who will later be killed; he studies Voltaire; he falls in love with Viola, a young maiden; he encounters and foils a possible attack by Arab pirates; he even manages to organize the villagers to prevent forest fires in the Ligurian Riviera.

The sphere of the "fantastic" permeates the entire novel, so much so that Calvino, in one of the prefaces to the book, makes an explicit reference to *Alice in Wonderland* (1865) and *Baron Munchausen* (1785), defining *The Baron in the Trees* as a "fantasy literature novel." It should not be forgotten that this book, along with *The Cloven Viscount* from 1952 and *The Nonexistent Knight* from 1959, constitutes the body of

opposite page
Iwan Baan, *View from one of the towers of the Bosco Verticale*, Boeri Studio, Milan, Italy, 2014

his fairy tales, written at a time when he was preparing a lengthy essay on Italian fairy tales.

The introduction to the dimension of the fantastic always has a dual consequence: on the one hand, it unsettles us, overturns the paradigm, completely changes the way we think about ourselves; on the other hand, it asks the reader for complicity in accepting a logical discipline, albeit unreal: that of plausibility. Thus, as in the imaginary world that Calvino invites us to share, it must be rigorous, precise, and potentially possible. In a small book that is very dear to me, *The Fantastic: A Structural Approach to a Literary Genre* (1975), Tristan Todorov explains well what fantastic literature is and its effect of displacement: it is a way of narrating life that leads us to change our perspective of the world, somehow bringing about a substantial change in perspective.
But once we accept this displacement, once we become accomplices in a fantastic yet plausible situation, the narration is absolutely rigorous, it adheres to the conditions established by the author.
As Todorov says, "fantastic literature touches on the themes of perspective," the way we view the world, not only the "themes of discourse," those that concern how we communicate with others.
Indeed, *The Baron in the Trees* touches on the themes of perspective: Cosimo lives in the trees, and from the heights of the trees, through the leaves and branches, he leads us to look at the world—history, social relationships, everything that surrounds us—in a different way, from another perspective. Moreover, Cosimo truly encounters history: to give just one example, he encounters Napoleon Bonaparte and—while in the trees—experiences the post-revolutionary Jacobin atmosphere. But he sees everything from above; because Cosimo views the things of the world, the men and women of the world, through the perspective filter of the leaves of the plants.

The Baron in the Trees is a captivating novel for many reasons. I remember reading it as a teenager and being literally enchanted by it. Part of the reason was because the story is set in the Ligurian Riviera, in that part of the

Stefano Boeri Architetti with Trudo, Application of the Vertical Forest model to social housing, Eindhoven, Netherlands, 2021

coast where my family has roots. My grandparents come from Taggia and Badalucco, from that area of the Argentina Valley that extends to Triora and has Sanremo and Taggia as its arrival and departure points to the sea. Sanremo was Calvino's hometown; he was born in Havana, Cuba, but spent his youth in Sanremo, a place that until World War II had an international and glamorous allure. Thanks to the presence of the Casinò, Sanremo was a meeting place for European high society, as well as the Italian landing point for a network of European intellectuals, including Calvino's father, a renowned botanist who had opened an international school in Sanremo.

But another aspect that gradually drew me into the plot of *The Baron in the Trees* is the sophisticated and powerful way in which Calvino brings out the features of the Ligurian Riviera in his novel. Calvino never uses a detailed description of the geography of the landscape; instead, he evokes some traces of it. Yet, it is impossible not to enter the imaginary world of this unique space, populated by the sea, forests, and stories of life, intense, very intense emotional relationships.

Perhaps the memory of such a reading experience evoking a geographical space to me led to my interest in exploring the relationship between architecture and literature—a fascinating and challenging theme.
A few years ago, when I was the director of the *Abitare* magazine, I, along with Gianluigi Ricuperati, attempted to involve writers in narrating the architectural works we published. We asked Bruce Sterling to imagine constructing a story within a house designed by François Roche in France. Ricky Moody was asked to imagine a story set in Sejima's New Museum in New York—and we did the same with Enrique Vila-Matas, Gonzalo Garcés, and other writers who narrated a space by localizing their literary imagination within it.
These were short stories where the environment emerged as atmosphere, through a series of clues. Moreover, I recently discussed this with Rem Koolhaas regarding the relationship between writing and architecture. I believe literature can express the sense of a space, the sense of a city, especially when it does not assign a leading role to this space, to this city, immediately visible.
The city emerges more forcefully when it remains in the background of the literary text, not immediately in view.
It's the same way the Ligurian Riviera, that fundamental part of Liguria, emerges in *The Baron in the Trees* and in many other novels or stories by Italo Calvino: space and the city emerge as a sort of unconscious that lies in the background of every narrated action. Without lengthy descriptions, yet with incredible expressive power.

The Baron in the Trees keeps resurfacing in my life.

It returned when I began to design the Bosco Verticale in Milan. And it returned when, a few years ago, I started to think about the vision of a Forest City—or the possibility of establishing a new balance between cities and forests.

At times, I come to think that the Bosco Verticale resembles an attempt, whether successful or not, to transpose within a building, within architecture, precisely this extraordinary botanical metamorphosis that Calvino proposes: a world, a city, a society, viewed through the perspective of oaks, cork oaks, holm oaks, olive trees, beech trees, and chestnut trees.

After all, this is what is produced in the Bosco Verticale every day: we look at the world from the tops of the branches, through the leaves; it's a viewpoint that implies a substantial shift in the visual paradigm, just as it happens in fantastic literature.

Here, the botanical world, which we usually place within a garden, confine in a park, keep away in a forest, is indeed the first filter through which we view the world. We introduce into the vision of a city that elsewhere—the living, untamed nature—that we usually attempt to conceive "outside" our habitat.

With the Bosco Verticale, I unconsciously sought to give physicality, tactile and sensory experience to the literary imagery unleashed by *The Baron in the Trees*. Albeit in the opposite direction, this is something that resembles the attempts made with *Abitare* to restore the characteristics of an inhabited space through literary narration. Also because, like from the windows of the Bosco Verticale, Cosimo looks at life through the life of the trees; his is not a simple zenithal vision that flattens things, removes shadows and thicknesses. On the contrary, it is a way of looking at the world as if it were in axonometry: you see the shadows, the thicknesses of things and people, but through the mediation of the leaves and the filter of the branches.

The ending of *The Baron in the Trees* is poignant: Biagio Piovasco di Rondò, Cosimo's brother, recounts Cosimo's death. Cosimo, old and very ill, beloved by the citizens who are standing under the tree on which he is dying, suddenly sees a hot-air balloon passing by, piloted by English aeronauts. To everyone's amazement, he grabs onto a rope dangling from the balloon and

Italo Calvino, *Baron in the Trees* (London: Collins, 1959). Cover by Domenico Gnoli

opposite page Boeri Studio, Bosco Verticale, Milan, Italy, 2014

disappears. He vanishes into the sky, into the sea, into the gulf of Sanremo/ Rondò, and thus dies. He consummates his death in an invisible dimension. On his tomb, Biagio recalls "Cosimo Piovasco di Rondò—Lived in the trees—Always loved the earth—Ascended to heaven."

The last, beautiful words of the book are these:

"Ombrosa is no more. Looking at the clear sky I wonder if it really existed, those jagged branches and leaves, bifurcations, lobes, endless and minute down feathers, and the sky in irregular, cut-out patches. Perhaps it was only there so my brother could pass through it, with his light snipe-like step; it was an embroidery made on nothing that resembles this thread of ink, as I let it run for pages and pages, packed with deletions, references, nervous scribbles, stains, gaps that sometimes break into large clear clusters or sometimes densify into tiny dots like seed points, now twisting back on itself, now bifurcating, now connecting clumps of sentences with outlines of leaves or clouds. And then it stops, and then it resumes, twisting and running. It unravels and encompasses a last senseless cluster of words, ideas, and dreams, and it's over."[1]

1 Italo Calvino, *Il barone rampante,* Oscar Moderni (Milan: Mondadori, 2022), 246. Our translation.

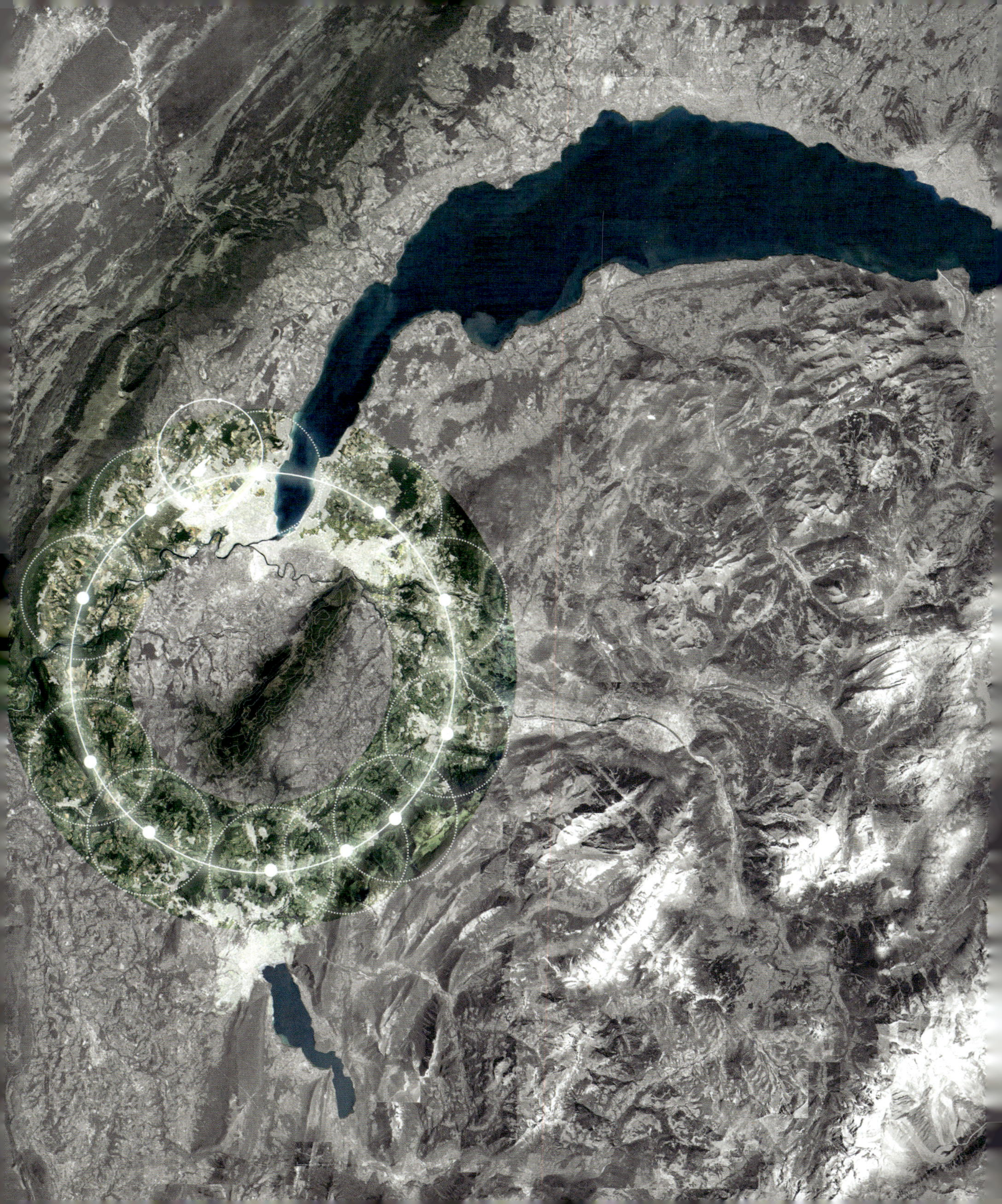

Vivre Ensemble
Antidotes to the anti-city

Stefano Boeri

Thirteen years ago, in a book titled *L'Anticittà* (2011), I reflected on the contemporary city and the controversial issue of urban sprawl, asking myself what a city is to me. The truth is that I can only answer this question negatively, by explaining what a city definitely is not, or rather, what it should never be.

A city is not merely a place where like-minded individuals gather together; it is not a continuous sprawl of buildings, without a center and an end.

What distinguishes a city from any other piece of inhabited land is the unique relationship that is created between a community that hosts people with different origins, cultures, traditions, and needs, and the shape of the space that this community inhabits; a shape that becomes all the more compact and defined in its proportions and geometries, transforming itself into a shared identity and a space for the flow of individuals' lives. There is no city without a collective imagination capable of thinking of it and perceiving it as the common horizon of everyday life.

This relationship between the density of built spaces and the variety of cultures of those who inhabit them and feel represented by them—a topic largely explored by Jane Jacobs in her milestone book *The Death and Life of Great American Cities* (1961)—creates that "city effect," that cohesive urban community which, on the contrary, disappear if the intensity of one of the two terms decreases.

The dilution of urban intensity—meaning the loss of building density and, at the same time, the reduction of social variety among inhabitants—is at the root of the phenomenon of dispersion and negation of urban life, which I defined as the "anti-city." When the density of spaces decreases, the opportunities for social interaction and exchange that

opposite page
Stefano Boeri Architetti, Vision for a Metropolitan Constellation, Geneva, Switzerland, 2020

a city should offer diminish; when the variety of cultures diminishes, social homogenization prevails, with individuals and families of the same origin, culture, traditions, and needs concentrated in certain parts of the city. This leads to the formation of enclaves rather than a city.

If we want now to focus on the relationship between individuals and communities, between solitude and sociability, *Comment vivre ensemble* (1977) is an essential read: fourteen seminars that Roland Barthes held at the Collège de France, collected in an issue of the journal *Riga* in 2010.

People live together because they occupy the same space but, as Barthes writes, "they also live together from a chronological point of view, in the contemporaneity of living."

How can solitary life and collective life be held together? How can the experience that follows the individual rhythm be harmonized with that which follows the collective rhythm and the inclusive experience of others? According to Barthes, the monks who lived on Mount Athos, an extraordinary place overlooking the Mediterranean, had achieved an *idiorrhythmic* balance—the harmonious combination of the need for a solitary life that could still open up to community life. "It is not a utopia, because what I am pursuing is not a social dimension but an almost domestic dimension . . . if anything, it is a domestic utopia that I am pursuing."

This harmony between individual and collective life cannot be resolved with utopian discourse but requires reflection based on the practices of daily life.

In recent decades, many thinkers and scholars have addressed these themes, relating them to urban forms of sociality.

I would like to mention three of them, in a non-chronological order.

The first is Edward T. Hall, whose two books—*The Silent Language* in 1959 and *The Hidden Dimension* in 1966—laid the foundations of proxemics, a discipline that gained significant success in the 1960s, especially in the fields of semiology and semiotics. Proxemics also en-

gaged the knowledge of ethnology, ecology, anthropology, sociology, and design.
The aim of proxemics is the study of gestures, behaviors, spaces, and distances in communication, both verbal and non-verbal. Hall distinguished several types of distance: personal distance, which is between two individuals; domestic distance, which is more complex as it is measured by a system of interrelations, typically familial ones; and social distance, which concerns the positioning of bodies in relation to urban spaces and the flow of movement within a territory or city. Hall interacted with Italian semiologists—particularly Umberto Eco and Paolo Fabbri—as well as architects like Vittorio Gregotti. Refocusing on proxemics, analyzing the multiple forms of distancing and rapprochement of bodies, is, in my opinion, of paramount importance.

The second author is Robert Putnam, an important figure in the history of Northern American urban sociology.
In 2000, Putnam wrote *Bowling Alone*, a stark examination of the explosion of loneliness as a mass phenomenon in US society. In this book, Putnam provides a very interesting definition of the concept of "social capital," which is not measurable quantitatively but is nonetheless a form of wealth, consisting of the network of social connections and norms of reciprocity and trust that each individual or social group possesses.
Putnam distinguishes between two main forms of social capital: "bonding social capital" and "bridging social capital." The former is the capital that allows the formation of an identity bond. Bonding social capital includes everything that, starting from the ties and traditions passed down by the family, helps to strengthen one's identity in relation to another: traditions, expectations, culture, religious beliefs. The other form of social capital, bridging social capital, allows us to enrich our culture through exchange with those who have different origins, cultures, faiths, languages, and behaviors.
Putnam tells us how these two modalities must continually interact and are both necessary within a community. Without the first, the

minimal conditions to accept exposing one's identity to the risk of exchange with others are not in place. But without the second, one loses the opportunity to enrich one's identity through interaction with others and by assuming their perspective on the world.
I believe that, in rethinking collective spaces, urban planning and architecture should understand what it can mean to identify and design this relationship between bridging and bonding social capital in the spaces of our cities.

Richard Sennett, an American sociologist and anthropologist, has worked extensively on the concept of the "open city." I have had the opportunity to discuss this with him several times; his idea is of a city with porous boundaries, where citizens intermingle, learning to manage the complexity of urban living.
In his book, *Building and Dwelling* (2018), which focuses on the relationship between building and living in cities, Sennett explains: "Building means affirming values that the community may not wish to have. It sometimes implies imposing justice on the community, even though the tension between building and dwelling will always be present."
For Sennett, an open city is indeed a city that accepts the risk of exchange and incorporates a plural system of communities into its fabric. This can succeed to the extent that the importance of bonding social capital is recognized.

The last author I want to mention is Edouard Glissant, a writer, poet, essayist, and sociologist who has worked on the boundary between assimilation and local identity.
After initially adhering to the thesis of *Negritude*, Glissant developed the concept of *Antillanité*, based on the idea that it is possible to develop a multiple identity in contemporary society. The question Glissant posed is the possibility of protecting a very strong cultural tradition—which has ancient roots but arose from colonialism, slavery, and a reinterpretation of local cultures—while also accepting the challenge of assimilation and cultural integration without any naivety. Moving

along this boundary, Glissant developed the concept of *mondialité*, which identifies a fertile relationship between the archipelago of individualities and the vast sea of collectivity.
On another level, Saskia Sassen recognises a few 'global cities' as having the power to direct the flows of an almost totally interconnected planet. *Mondialité* contrasts with globalization: "It is not true that the only way to perceive the openness of the world is through technocratic globalization, the expansion of information networks, ideas, and goods across the entire planet. There is a *mondialité*, a dimension of worldliness in every local space, there is a dimension of the world's complexity in every country, in every village, in every city. . . and this mondialité is a condition of contemporaneity that we have everywhere."

It may be useful today to revisit Barthes—and invoke authors such as Putnam, Sennett, and Glissant—as the question of "living together" presents us with significant challenges.
The first concerns our relationship with the other, those different from us. Starting from Putnam's considerations, we should ask ourselves what is the minimum identity necessary to accept the risk of exchange with the other. At the same time, we should also ask ourselves what is the minimum exchange with the other necessary to enrich and strengthen an identity that would otherwise remain closed in on itself, becoming self-referential. This challenge must also be translated into the design of living spaces, from the domestic scale to that of the housing unit, the block, the neighborhood, and the entire city.
Whatever discussions we may have about the future of our cities, we cannot, under any circumstances, abandon their openness, our neighborhoods, our social relationships, as Sennett suggests.
But let us not be deceived into thinking that this is achievable digitally: in exchange and in the social capital of exchange, there are indeed a series of values that are linked to proxemics, the silent language of bodies, gestures, and attitudes. We need this as much as we need food: we need physical interaction, spatial interaction.
The second challenge is the one I mentioned when quoting Glissant:

there is a wealth of mondialité in every space, in every place, in every neighborhood: today, our cities are world-cities. The world can inhabit the local, the everyday circuits, our countries.
And finally, the third challenge, perhaps the most important: it is the open public space that nurtures collective life; we cannot afford to accept barriers, even invisible ones, to our need for connections.

In our work as designers, we should constantly reflect on how the spaces and objects of our lives can contribute to achieving the right balance between the two forms of social capital—the strength of identity and the necessity of difference—spoken of by Putnam. And how our projects can generate positive effects on the strengthening of community relationships over time and not just in space.
We must think about how design can truly become the creative engine for an open city, a world-city where global energies converge.

Stefano Boeri Architetti, The walkable Red Circle and the wind turbine tower, Genoa, Italy, 2019

opposite page
Stefano Boeri Architetti, The Polcevera Park and the Red Circle master plan designed after the collapse of the Morandi Bridge, Genoa, Italy, 2019

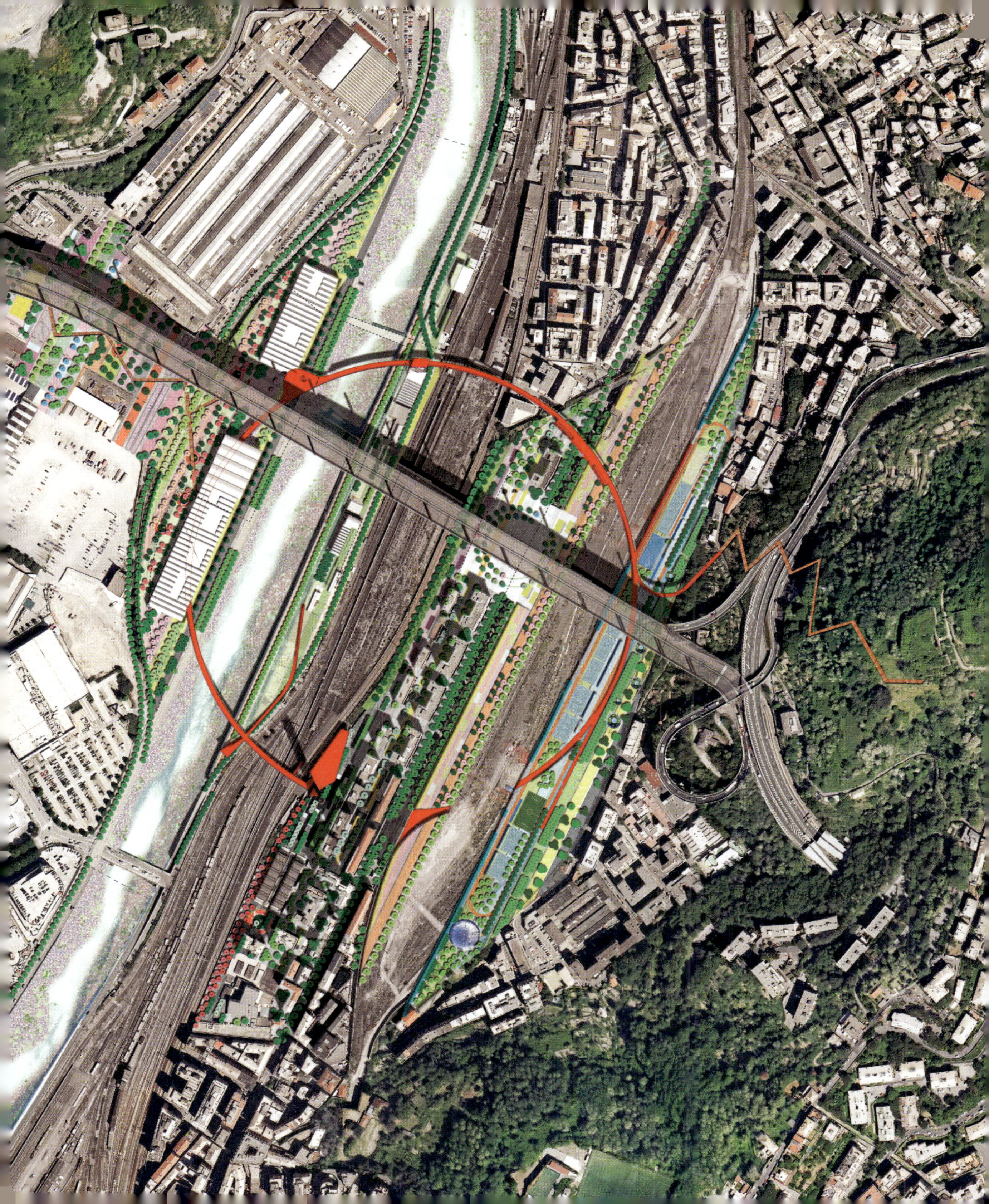

Field Diary (1982). A diary shot in the occupied territories before and during the 1982 Lebanon war

Modern Fetish

Shielded by a camera

Amos Gitai

The camera is a kind of fetish. It is not just a reproducing machine, capable of replicating movement, color, and texture alongside a sound recording device. It's a machine that, in the second half of the twentieth century, acquired the power of a ceremonial object, whose very presence allows filmmakers to enter places they wouldn't have access to without it. I would never have been able to board Rabin's plane or enter the White House (*Give Peace a Chance*, 1994) to see and try to understand what interested me if I hadn't had this fetish in my hands. Now, one can say that the camera holds the power of a pagan fetish. Many believe in its ability to change seasons, move objects, and trigger events. A person's willingness to be in or excluded from the recorded image by the camera lens is determined by belief in this power; the unlimited capacity for reproduction and dissemination of the filmed image is one of the elements that give this medium its political dimension.

Let's not forget that the camera frames. Filming involves making a series of decisions that determine not only what will be included in the frame but also what will not. This means that our choices involve a degree of distancing and marginalization. The camera, like cinema, produces a subjective document. It expresses a particular point of view.

These factors require reflection on the appropriate filming strategy for each film and the particular, measured use that will be made of this fetish called a camera. In an era where we are bombarded with television images, whether it's news or entertainment programs, where technology and the image production industry continue to progress and become more sophisticated, it's important to remain acutely aware of the act of representation; to keep in mind that it's not just about "what" to film, that is, the content of the produced image, but "how" to film, that is, the technique or, if you will, the procedures for producing the images. This aesthetic concept is present in most of my films.

I must reflect on the meaning or cultural function of the tools and materials with which I work in the context that is mine. This is precisely why, when filming, one must think about camera strategies, about the kind of gaze one wants to bring. These aspects obviously fall under an ethics of the relationship between the camera and the filmed object.
I would formulate it as follows: between a person or object being filmed and a director or filmmaker, there is always a kind of contract that implies that both parties are aware of the act of filming. The concept of "cinéma vérité," which the French managed to impose at a certain time, is very misleading. This "truth," if it exists, is nothing more than a series of perspectives, the sum of which perhaps constitutes "something." The illusion that the camera can pivot on its axis and transmit reality as it is, in my opinion, is one of the most deceptive ideas in cinema. I don't believe in hidden cameras; the camera is an object that must be exposed. In some cases, it must be extremely visible, and in others, it needs to be revealed differently.
People's resistance to the recording form the camera wishes to undertake is an integral part of the project. And their reservations about what I do or say during filming must remain in the film: through these reservations, they mark the boundaries they wish to establish and participate in formulating the tacit contract between the documenter and the documented. These boundaries are not only interesting, they are important and are even a matter of principle insofar as they define, perhaps with extreme precision, the ability or inability of cinema to record "slices of reality."
The presence of the camera in a documentary situation always raises a question: do we want it to function as a weapon, as in *Field Diary* (1982), where it registers resistance to the recording process, and the relationships and power balances at the time of filming? Do we want it to have a discreet presence, as in *Wadi* (1981), where everyone filmed was aware of being filmed and sometimes objected to this continuous recording, asked for it to stop but without questioning the recording process itself, the physical presence of the camera object itself? Do we want to proceed as in *Bangkok–Bahrein* (1984), where the camera tries to "contain" a man and a woman who trade Thai workers they export to Gulf countries and where the camera movements expose unexpected facets of their relationships? Or perhaps, as in the case of

In the Valley of the Wupper (1994), we want to film (deliberately without lighting) the prosecutor of the Wuppertal region who, when he sees the clapperboard and the light arrive, asks "Are you starting to film?" and whose speech changes, meaning that the camera records both situations and what differentiates them.

The scene from *In the Valley of the Wupper* in which I talk with passersby in a street in Wuppertal, for example, is entirely constructed based on how the camera's eye is positioned in relation to the object being filmed. My basic decision was as follows: the passersby are filmed on the sidewalk in front of a skinhead bar, but I don't place the camera on the sidewalk next to them; on the contrary, I place it across the street, and the traffic of cars that occasionally interrupts us does the "editing" of the filmed objects. The microphone is not placed near the bar wall; sometimes, it is next to the camera. This geometry in space, with the traffic of cars (which I chose not to interrupt), indicates to us that it's a normal situation, that meeting these passersby outside the bar is nothing exceptional, that it's a new slice of life captured in a film, that life continues to flow in the bar while we chat outside. This creates the rhythm of the scene: the distance and absence of familiarity between the director and his camera and the filmed object. One must be aware of these aspects when shooting.

In other situations, it's about creating an almost intimate relationship between the camera and the filmed object. When I made *Wadi* in 1981 for example, I asked the cameraman, Yossi Wein, not to use a tripod and to put a scarf on the ground to place the camera, in order to create a sense of closeness with those being filmed. I didn't want them to perceive the fetish of being filmed as a distant threat but rather as an object among others in their environment: there's a cup, a chair, a bottle, and there's also a camera. I also asked that the camera remain completely static, without any choreography. I just wanted those speaking elements that reveal characters to be in the frame. When I returned to film in the same place ten years later, in 1991, with Nurith Aviv, who is a master of camera movement, I told her: "This time, don't move the camera at all. You choose its location, we look together to choose the frame, we place the person in that frame, and that's it. That's the film."

When I filmed *Field Diary*, on the other hand, I wanted the camera to create the unity of time, the chapters of this diary, in a fluidity with the filmed object, in order to delineate the space and context of the occupation. In this case, the camera does the opposite of what it does in *Wadi*, among other things, because of its presence: it's no longer a camera timidly placed on the ground on a scarf but an aggressive, wary, and even malicious camera, carried on the shoulder, giving the impression of wanting to push the filmed object out of its personal space, and when the latter resists, there's a struggle. Will the camera succeed in recording its object on film, or will the soldiers, strawberry growers, and others succeed in preventing the act of filming? The struggle takes place on the lens of the camera: that's where the conflict occurs.

I like to use different filming strategies depending on the film, whether it's a documentary or fiction.

Take the case of *Kadosh* (1999). As soon as I understood the parameters of the film, I chose to move away from its place of origin, an ultra-Orthodox neighborhood in Jerusalem, and to film most of the scenes in places that are not where the plot unfolds. I felt it was important not to provoke conflict about the necessities of the shooting itself, that it wasn't even appropriate at all in the case of this film. A fiction film must preserve its space to be able to raise questions that direct confrontation with reality doesn't allow to formulate. Fiction cinema is architectural. It builds or rebuilds what doesn't exist beforehand. It's the making of a trompe l'oeil; while documentary cinema, as far as I'm concerned, is archaeological: it digs. It tries to expose hidden states, previous layers—whether it's an obscure social structure or a skeleton buried just below the surface.

In documentary, the relationships between the filmmaker filming and the filmed object are crucial. They must be explicitly present in the film and shed light on the meaning of what we see. This is true for *Field Diary*, where we are witnesses, in the literal sense of the word, of the hand holding the camera; it is also true for Wadi, where Miriam or Skandar ask to stop the camera; and it's true for *In the Valley of the Wupper* and *Bangkok–Bahrein*.

A fiction film is, for me, a kind of allegory. Sometimes, in the final sequences, I expose the moment when I am making the film. The filmmaker's intervention in shaping the film becomes apparent in the work itself, making the viewer aware of the film's space and time of production—a gesture arising from the collision between allegorical narrative and the filming context, as well as from the desire to use this collision as a filmmaking tool. Some situations justify this relationship being exposed.

Very often, my films expose traces of my interventions, both in documentaries and fiction. Sometimes, the camera draws the viewer's gaze in a direction opposite to what they are supposed to see. It's about naming the act of filming and making the audience aware of the existence of different surfaces. I also do this on the soundtracks of many films.

Fiction and documentary are different territories, in my opinion. Everyone who makes documentaries knows that they can find themselves in situations that appear to be fiction or worse, that would be considered unbelievable if they were fictional. For me, this doesn't change the necessity of protecting the specificity of a documentary film. And even though it's possible to apply the techniques and working strategies of one genre to the other, the differences between them must be preserved and even accentuated. Documentary cinema deals with the representation of reality; this doesn't mean that fiction films don't do the same, but they do it with different materials, discourse, and aims. In documentary cinema, we deal with real people and situations that happen in reality. The complexity of the set of variables we have to manage requires clear rules. That's why, in general, I prefer to dig and expose the archaeological layers of delimited sites, where it's easier to observe the exact geometry of the relationships they present, rather than making general statements. Since it's about reality, I prefer to limit myself to telling the story of a house, a box of pineapples, a valley, or a particular event, as in Wuppertal.

For me, the long take is one of the most subversive cinematic means. This type of shot makes it possible to create a rhythm that forces the viewer to adopt a different gaze, one that doesn't correspond to the mechanical gaze we've been accustomed to by TV series or reports, and even by commercial cinema. Extending the duration raises questions for the viewer. When a shot extends beyond the conventional place or duration, when we force the viewer to stay, to continue watching the image, they are obliged to realize it and become aware of the questions it raises.

In general, I believe that any form of cinema that includes the awareness of the film's duration by the viewer attempts to preserve a certain degree of complexity in presenting a problem. Duration allows another gaze to be recorded. This is based on a series of assumptions, which I will try to define. Modern reality is a fragmented, disjointed reality. I believe that the main experience of modernity is that of uprooting, migration, and exile. Most of the societies we live in are made up of people who have migrated from one place to another. Israel is one of the products of these exiles, with people coming from Central and Eastern Europe, North Africa, Ethiopia, not to mention Palestinians who have been exiled by Israelis. For this society entirely composed of uprooted residents (except perhaps those born there), it's actually nothing extraordinary. This is a typical phenomenon of the twentieth century. Reality, no matter how we look at it, isn't coherent—whether architecturally, socially, economically, or culturally. It doesn't even offer the illusion of unity: it's no longer the distant reality of a unified past by tradition, where the individual was part of a community, a succession of generations living in a continuum one after the other—it's a broken reality, completely fragmented.

An individual's life experience in this broken reality is that of a stranger, of coincidence, of alienation, and of chance encounters. The experience offered by modern culture is that of juxtaposition—a sort of discontinuous neighborhood of slices of reality, a proximity that places people next to each other, leading them to attribute things to each other that don't belong or correspond to them. Detaching a form from its context and placing it in another context is not new: it's a central theme of twentieth-century art. That's why I think that the only way to use modern experience is to contain it in a given space. When we experience everyday life on a bus or in a car—the vehicles through which we experience the urban landscape in which we live, whether in Tel Aviv, Cairo, Amman, Ramallah, or Manila—the continuity of this movement through these spaces encompasses for us, subjectively, a series of impressions, movements, and experiences. It's not very different from the literary means used by writers like James Joyce in *Dubliners*, for example, or by Yaakov Shabtai in *Past Perfect*, novels in which they try to deal with the question of the temporal proximity of a series of fragments. I think that the duration created by the movement of the camera in a long take—which brings together and connects series of fragments—is a response to this problem in terms of cinema, to a certain extent.

In my work, not only is the long take of a different nature in each film, but its purpose also differs. In documentary films such as *Field Diary*, it aims to keep a record of time and even stretch it to its real dimension, instead of shortening it through an act of editing that condenses and compresses the temporal framework. It's a kind of suspicion that means: before you stands the continuous and complete temporal framework as it is, containing such and such contradictions, which I present to you without making cuts. Look and judge for yourselves. And since the camera is in motion in this shot, which can last up to seven or ten minutes, you can see the space in a single movement of almost 360 degrees, and the event itself will be transmitted to you at the pace at which it occurred, without any intervention on my part. Of course, I can change the camera's focal length, but I will not change or accelerate anything.

In *Berlin–Jerusalem*, which is a fiction film, the long take has entirely different meanings. The film consists of drawing two trajectories, one of the poet Else Lasker-Schüler, who travels from Berlin to Jerusalem, and the other of Manya Shohat, who left Russia to found the first kibbutzim. The structure of the film is an interweaving: from Berlin to Palestine, from Palestine to Berlin, until the final shot, where we arrive in Israel. The Berlin shots are a tribute to expressionist painting, while the kibbutz scenes are reminiscent of socialist realism pamphlets.

The final shot is a passage through time. It begins with the narrative continuum of fiction, that of a "historical" film set in the thirties and forties, and ends at the time the filming took place: 1988–89. This means that the shot depicts a transition of fifty years in a few minutes. We move from those who arrived in Palestine in the thirties and forties, with radiant utopian ideas, to the time of the first Intifada in the late eighties. This shot does exactly the opposite of that in *Field Diary*: it's a montage gesture that focuses on sound rather than image.

Filmed continuously, without cuts, the sequence compresses fifty years into a single temporal frame of seven minutes. The reuse of voice fragments taken from the soundtrack and placed in a new context creates a contrast between historical time and cinematic time. This camera movement, which is also a movement through time, and this associative reuse of voices from the past allow us to examine the absurdity of the contradictions of Zionist ideology.

For the birthday dinner scene of Hanna in *Yom Yom* (1998), the significance of the long take is different. This time, it's about the continuous rotation of the camera on the tripod axis. The camera movements seem to follow the lines of Mimi (Keren Mor), which are apparently what transition her from one character to another. But sometimes the camera prefers to wander in a completely subjective, undisciplined, or even random way before returning to Mimi's face. It's never mechanical. In each film, and sometimes even in different shots of the same film, I try to take advantage of the varied possibilities offered by this technique.

In *Field Diary*, the seven-minute long take follows a small group of soldiers in Ramallah and exposes the relationship between the film crew and them. It can be formulated as follows: a group of soldiers walks in Ramallah in search of a boy who threw stones at them, in order to interrogate him. The presence of the camera—according to them—prevents them from doing so. That is to say, here, cinema engages not only in documenting reality but also in engaging with reality by intervening in it. The camera, which is involved in the scene, changes something in the scene. On the one hand, this act of documenting prevents a violent act that would have occurred if the camera had not been there. On the other hand, three soldiers are chased away from where they are sitting because they do not want to be filmed. But here, the soldiers are not trying to directly prevent filming. They radio their commander to tell him that there has been a man driving around the corner in his car for half an hour, and they ask for directions. These directions, although we cannot hear them and we do not know exactly what they consist of, seem to be something like "Get out of there." Which means that the act of filming has produced something unique: it made the army leave. Throughout this maneuver, viewers are constantly aware of the relationships between the film crew and the soldiers. My harassing presence, as a director, is constantly felt, and viewers know how and to what extent the director bothers the soldiers. Seeing and being seen, like the act of filming itself, are integral parts of the film and its discourse.

Amos Gitai, *Architecture de la mémoire*, installation at Église des Frères-Prêcheurs, Rencontres photographiques d'Arles, France, July 2 – September 23, 2012

following pages
Meital Barda and Yael Abecassis in *Kadosh* (1999). The life of two sisters in an ultra-Orthodox neighborhood in Jerusalem

ATECO
K INDUSTRY

Others

For a non-anthropocentric urban ethics

Stefano Boeri

The breaking of a cohabitation pact among living species is at the root of spillover processes, the overflow of a virus from one animal species to our own. This highly topical issue has been present for years in numerous scientific studies and was also addressed in a book written in 2012 by American science journalist David Quammen. Quammen's book, *Spillover: Animal Infections and the Next Human Pandemic*, which anticipated the pandemic scenario that has exploded around the world in recent years, limpidly describes the causes of zoonotic processes. About 60% of infectious diseases come from incongruous contact with wild animals, the onset of pandemics being related to deforestation. In fact, deforestation not only affects the habitat of the viruses themselves, which are forced to find other means of survival (like other vehicles of transmission) but above all, it drastically reduces the biodiversity present in a forest or woodland and thus resets to zero the countless species transitions that a virus must normally make before it reaches ours.

The truth is that in recent decades, by upsetting ancient balances as a result of out-of-control urbanization, we have continued to take away space from the lives of other animal species.

Every time we replace a piece of forest with a piece of city, with a monocultural growing area or intensive farming, when we force non-domestic species into captivity (as is often the case in slums and in some of the poorest areas of the world's metropolises), we change the balance among living species. As a result of our tendency to destroy the natural habitats of other species and constrain them to forced and coercive cohabitation, the balance is now broken. We are actually undoing the richness and variety not only of plant biodiversity, but also of the animal life of which we are a part.

opposite page
Pieter Hugo, *The Hyena Men of Nigeria*, Abuja, 2007

In the latest season of *Planet Earth* (2016), the BBC's documentary series, particularly in the episode *Cities*, dedicated to the explosion of metropolises, David Attenborough documents the coexistence of humans, felines, and predators: a leopard chasing wild boars at night in the middle of the slums of Mumbai, hyenas prowling the streets in search of food, hawks flying over New York. Think of the news published in *The Guardian* during the lockdown about an invasion of monkeys: accustomed to living in a small Thai community and orphaned by visitors, these monkeys became aggressive and entered the central spaces of the city in search of food. And again: we know that, in northern countries, due to the effects of global warming on their habitat, for a long time polar bears have been seeking food elsewhere, progressively approaching populated areas.

But the now visible signs of forced cohabitation are not only to be found in the large megacities of China or the favelas of South America or South-East Asia. Forced cohabitation with other non-domestic species is something we are also experiencing in the cities of the Western world, in our daily urban life. The question we should ask ourselves today is therefore how to find a balance in the coexistence of different species; it is a balance, however, that should not be imposed according to the same forms of aggression that paradoxically facilitated the emergence and explosion of Covid-19 around the world.

Jane Goodall's work teaches us a vision of biodiversity that is not only about recognizing the cohabitation of different species but, above all, acknowledging the possibility of coexistence among diverse *intelligences*. This is a fundamental step because, by recognizing the cognitive abilities and emotional lives of non-human beings, she calls into question humanity's perceived dominion over the natural world, urging us to adopt a non-anthropocentric stance toward all living creatures. It holds us, as the dominant species, responsible for understanding and respecting the needs of these other intelligences, which are interrelated in a system of continuous exchange.

The great challenge in the coming decades will be to quickly learn to come down from our pedestal as a hegemonic species and take on the point of view of other species, to consider their intelligence and sensitivity. And, at the same time, not abdicating our responsibility for the destructive and self-destructive

processes we have caused and are responsible for, starting with the issue of global warming. We should take on the enormous responsibility for having produced an imbalance where a previous balance existed, commit ourselves to bringing back cohabitation where we have brought conflict and destruction. We should study the living spaces of other species and understand how to respect them, even within our own privileged habitat built over the centuries: cities. We are doing this with plant species; we can also do it with animal species, starting with those that, while remaining wild, share city space with us.
In taking on the perspective of other animal species, we must recognize their intelligence as undoubtedly different but no less structured than ours: there is, to give an example, sophisticated intelligence in the functional logic that guides the life of ants, or in the affective relationships of dolphins. There is memory and sensitivity in the life choices of a crow, as Konrad Lorenz told us years ago in *King Solomon's Ring* (1949), but also more recently by scholars Bert Hölldobler and Edward O. Wilson in *Journey to the Ants: A Story of Scientific Exploration* (1994), and with them many other popularizers and experts. Intelligence is not a map, but a kaleidoscope.
Just as in a forest there are networks of relationships and balances of mutual rescue between plants and animals, we should strive, even in the urban world, to rebuild a form of cohabitation and respect between different species.
Fifteen years ago, with Andrea Branzi, we attempted to explore the concept of a new anthropocentrism in a project for Grand Paris. On the model of India's great metropolises, we tried to imagine new forms of unforced coexistence between humans and animals in the heart of Paris. Coexistence with large mammals, birds, rodents: the idea was that Paris would become the first metropolis in the world to get rid of an anthropocentric urban ethics. This is a theme that is dear to my heart and one I also addressed in 2008 in *Abitare* no. 480, in an article titled "Down from the stand: Arguments in favour of a non-anthropised urban ethics," illustrated with drawings by Mario Piazza. It is a perspective that we have recently reproposed, with higher realism, in our project for Grand Genève, where the center of the new metropolitan constellation we hypothesized would become a mountain, the Salève, a place of free expression and circulation of the life of other living species.

REGIE: FEDERICO FELLINI
SCENARIO: FEDERICO FELLINI & BERNARDINO ZAPPONI
PROD: TURI VASILE
COPROD: ULTRA FILM ROME / LES PRODUCTIONS ARTISTES ASSOCIES PARIS
COULEURS · KLEUREN
DIST: VERD: ARTISTES ASSOCIES

Rome

Archipelago metropolis

Stefano Boeri

A massive phenomenon of built dispersion occurred in Europe and Italy starting from the mid-1970s, leading to the proliferation of "anti-cities" of single-family houses, apartment buildings, warehouses, shopping centers, and car washes. These are vast territories with low housing density and population, created by the clustering around major urban centers of a multitude of solitary buildings that had obliterated the boundaries between urban, suburban, rural, and natural areas, simply overlapping and ignoring them.

The anti-city, that incongruous crowd of built volumes that we have become accustomed to seeing pass by the window of a car or train when entering or leaving any Italian and European city, is precisely an urban configuration lacking a hierarchy between center and periphery, coherence between its parts, and a clear perimeter. It is an apparently illogical formation, created by the individual and uncoordinated actions of thousands of individuals, families, and groups given the opportunity to build their living space, but without any shared design, project, or vision of the city or community.

The anti-city represents the triumph of individualistic economic democracy, where the right to modify space at one's discretion prevails without obligations. It creates a social landscape that simultaneously produces a rarefaction of urban density and a powerful social homogenization, the exact opposite of the diverse and rich community that, cohabiting in a compact place, triggers relationships and creates a city.

To understand the evolution of a city means, in short, to observe the continuous state transitions that characterize the waves of expansion and retraction, condensation and dilution of human behaviors in space, and recording the friction these waves encounter on the built matter of the city.

opposite page
Belgian poster for *Roma*, directed by Federico Fellini, 1972

After the Covid-19 pandemics, we are witnessing a transformation of the urban fabric toward a more controlled building density, both in time and space, concentrated in neighborhoods or "urban villages," rather than in individual epicenters: in zones with variable density, rather than in building emergencies.

As architects, we should pay more attention to the enormous potential of a metropolis that has often been looked at with condescension in recent years, despite recognizing in Rome the beginnings of a new idea of what a city could become in the future. Rome is now a model to look at.
Why Rome, today, specifically?
If we think about the contemporary model of a large city composed of autonomous parts, where landscapes and environments are not squeezed onto one another but coexist with spaciousness, connected by parks, green corridors, and water systems, the mind inevitably turns to Rome.

Rome, which has expanded to become the largest agricultural municipality in Europe—with 50,000 hectares of cultivated areas within its boundaries out of a total of 85,000 hectares of green areas, almost 70% of the municipal territory—carries centuries of history that have left indelible marks, capable of continually resurfacing from every attempt at erasure. Often, it is precisely around these legacies of different historical epochs that extraordinary ecological niches have formed, where various plant and animal species coexist in quantities and varieties unknown to other cities in the world.

Rome is that part of human history where archaeology has intertwined with ethology, architecture with animal breeding, where the remains of the Forum were once a pasture, a "Campo Vaccino." It is the city where, in Caravaggio's time—as Roberto Longhi reminds us in his texts and exhibitions on seventeenth-century painting—flocks of sheep roamed the streets of the city center. Transhumance, the presence of exotic birds in the parks, the invasion of seagulls and cormorants ascending from the Tiber and settling on the Aniene, along with hedgehogs, wild boars, and

Stefano Boeri Interiors, The new southern entrance to the Colosseum, Rome, Italy, 2024

foxes that inhabit even central areas, are indispensable components of Rome's metropolitan landscape.

The 40 species of mammals, 16 species of reptiles, 10 species of amphibians, 5,200 species of insects, and 121 species of birds, often mentioned by ethologist Enrico Alleva, make Rome an environment rich in biodiversity and unique in the world.

Rome, a city that Fellini, walking through the immense avenues of the EUR district, called "the placenta of the world," is already an *archipelago metropolis*, despite its enormous governance problems, and represents an extraordinary reference for the future of cities worldwide.

If for no other reason, Rome simply is the world and therefore holds within it the entire future.

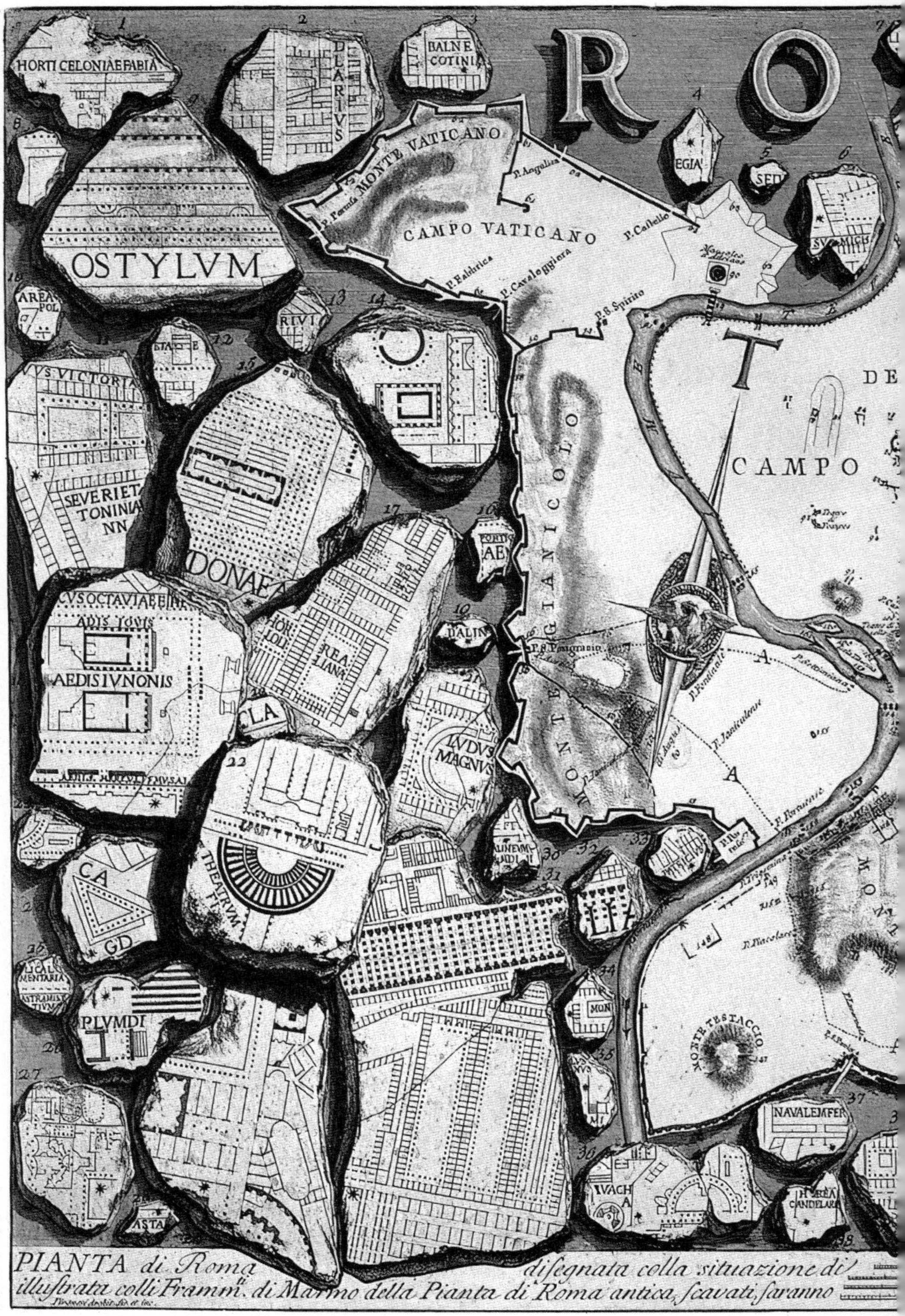

Giovanni Battista Piranesi (1720–1778), *Map of Rome*, in *Le Antichità Romane*, 1756

tutti i Monumenti antichi, de'quali in oggi ancora se ne vedono gli avanzi, ed
due secoli, nelle Rovine del Tempio di Romolo; ed ora esistenti nel Museo di Campidoglio.

Irène Jacob in *Why War* (2024), after the correspondence between Albert Einstein and Sigmund Freud in 1932

Form Meanings

The dialectics of form and narrative

Amos Gitai

Architecture is one of the oldest art forms because it concerns a fundamental human need; cinema, on the other hand, is superfluous. Architecture, like food production, military organization, and clothing, is one of the few essential needs human beings have had since the beginning of culture. Cinema is very recent. Its production methods are very similar to those of architecture, in the sense that they require the same simultaneous attention to the overall superstructure and to details. Just as in architecture, good buildings are not merely the result of good design or a good concept but require monitoring of the construction process and coordination of details, good films, regardless of the quality of the script, depend on the quality of lighting, editing, and movement choreography. Architecture and cinema are both a matter of rhythms and texts.

Neither architecture nor cinema are intimate arts. It's not like the painter in front of their canvas. People need to be mobilized. And in both mediums, it's about translating texts into forms. The architect receives a brief that specifies functions, budget, materials, etc., but they are just words that they must transform through the development of a form. A filmmaker works with a screenplay, and again, they are just words. The creative process of turning words into images is a similar procedure.

One of the reasons I did not pursue architecture is that, theoretically, this profession has become too obsessed with representation. Almost as if architects were jealous of filmmakers and often sought to produce images rather than buildings. For me, good architecture is not just about image. It's not just a graphic or design exercise. It needs, of course, to have an aesthetic visual aspect, but it must also consider spatial organization, circulation, access to transportation; that is, to integrate the way we compose our urban fabric. This approach is often absent today. Beautiful objects are built, reported in the news, but the real mission of architecture, which is much deeper, is not discussed. It's a commitment of a political nature, not just aesthetic or artistic.

I was also disappointed by the architectural process, which nowadays is hermetically sealed once the design phase is completed. Someone designs a building and someone else executes it. These two processes have become distinct from each other. In some of the great architectural successes, the design and production phases were often linked, to allow for the possibility of modifying the design throughout construction. This was valid for several reasons, including environmental reasons, which may be the most important. At Chartres, I can assume that the builders of the cathedral saw that there were very beautiful trees on the site and decided not to cut them down. There were also small hills. They didn't level them; they changed the orientation of the building. And this gives the positioning of this building in the landscape, in the context, all its grace. It's a process of adaptation and continuous dialogue with what exists and doesn't come from architects. It comes from elsewhere. From trees and hills. Current architects are often forced to work on a site without really considering the existing buildings, natural features, or the city. Building construction has become a closed process, an alienating process for workers and artisans. This dimension of adaptation to the environment, landscape, social needs, and political context is completely absent today, with few exceptions, due to the mode of fabrication. It's all about representation now (as Guy Debord theorized in his 1967 *The Society of the Spectacle*). In a certain type of cinema, you can maintain a craft process and continuously develop the project. Dialogue with the team helps rethink and evolve things. This interesting dynamic occurs in all my films.

The question is what the relationship between cinema and architecture, between cinema and shelter, can be. To begin to answer this, I will evoke the figure of my father, who was an architect trained at the Bauhaus, by showing you three letters, which in my opinion very simply explain the relationship between form and narrative, form and history, and architecture's attachment to form. The Bauhaus was created in 1919 in Weimar by Walter Gropius, immediately after the end of World War I—there is always a connection between politics, social and historical context, and architecture or art in general. This modernist, minimalist thinking, which sought transparency in architecture, was a kind of challenge to the subsequent Nazi architecture that emerged.

The first of these three letters was written by Mies van der Rohe to my father, who was then known as Munio Weinraub. Van der Rohe was one of the leading architects of the modernist movement in the twentieth century. This handwritten attestation dated August 7, 1931—before the Nazis came to power—documents that my father, who was 22 years old at the time, worked in his studio on one of his major projects. Let's observe the form of this letter. It is a very simple, minimalist letterhead, using only capital letters to indicate the name, Mies van der Rohe, the address—a single line of capitals, the date, and the recipient's name.

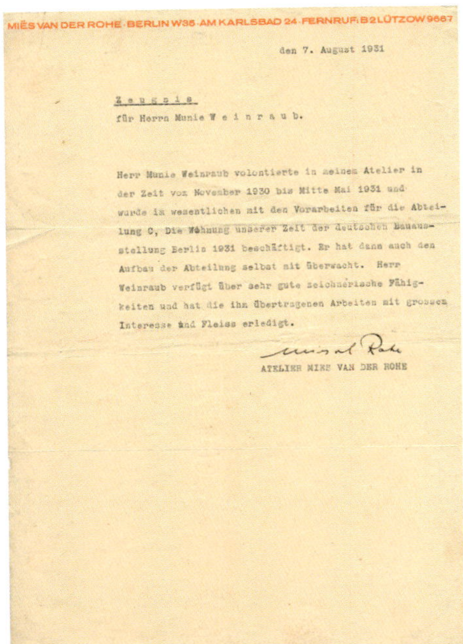
MIËS VAN DER ROHE · BERLIN W35 · AM KARLSBAD 24 · FERNRUF: B2 LÜTZOW 9667

den 7. August 1931

Z e u g n i s

für Herrn Munio W e i n r a u b.

Herr Munio Weinraub volontierte in meinem Atelier in der Zeit von November 1930 bis Mitte Mai 1931 und wurde im wesentlichen mit den Vorarbeiten für die Abteilung C, Die Wohnung unserer Zeit der deutschen Bauausstellung Berlin 1931 beschäftigt. Er hat dann auch den Aufbau der Abteilung selbst mit überwacht. Herr Weinraub verfügt über sehr gute zeichnerische Fähigkeiten und hat die ihm übertragenen Arbeiten mit grossem Interesse und Fleiss erledigt.

ATELIER MIES VAN DER ROHE

Certificate from Mies van der Rohe attesting that Munio Weinraub, the father of Amos Gitai, supervised the construction of the German Pavilion for the *Habitat of Our Time* exhibition, working in his studio from November 1930 to May 1931. Personal archives of Amos Gitai

The second letter, also signed by Mies van der Rohe, is written on Bauhaus letterhead in April 1932. My father is already a student in Dessau, where Gropius decided to move the school because of the Nazis' arrival in the Weimar City Council. These are small letters because the Bauhaus rejects the notion of hierarchy. That's why even typography is subject to very careful consideration.

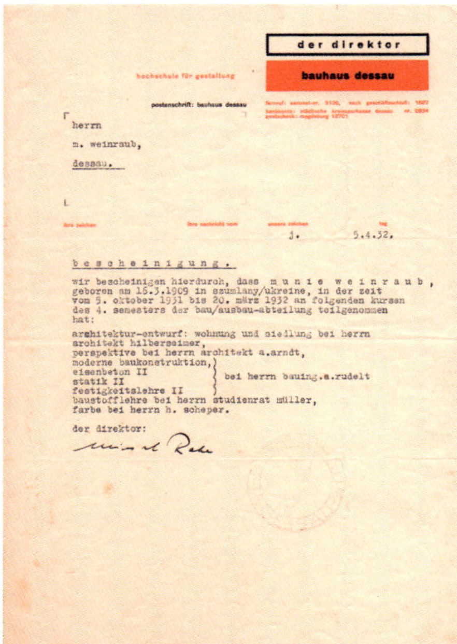
der direktor

hochschule für gestaltung

bauhaus dessau

postanschrift: bauhaus dessau

herrn

m. weinraub,

dessau.

j. 5.4.32.

bescheinigung.

wir bescheinigen hierdurch, dass munie weinraub, geboren am 15.3.1909 in szumlany/ukreine, in der zeit vom 5. oktober 1931 bis 20. märz 1932 an folgenden kursen des 4. semesters der bau/ausbau-abteilung teilgenommen hat:

architektur-entwurf: wohnung und siedlung bei herrn architekt hilberseimer,
perspektive bei herrn architekt a.arndt,
moderne baukonstruktion, eisenbeton II, statik II, festigkeitslehre II — bei herrn bauing.a.rudelt
baustofflehre bei herrn studienrat müller,
farbe bei herrn h. scheper.

der direktor:

Certificate from Mies van der Rohe, director of the Bauhaus, attesting that Munio Weinraub attended courses at the Bauhaus in Dessau from October 1931 to March 1932. Personal archives of Amos Gitai

Moving on to the third letter. We're in December 1933. Munio has already fled to Zurich after being imprisoned and beaten by the Nazis. The address is at the bottom left, and the letterhead uses gothic letters. Below the signature it says, "Heil Hitler!" We're used to hearing this in movies, accompanied by the Nazi salute . . . But here, it's written in black and white. The form is not neutral. Visually, it affirms a reference to a kind of Germanic kitsch romanticism, and the text tells Munio, who probably asked for a certificate of attendance for his years of study at the Bauhaus: "Excuse me, we have no record of your existence. Heil Hitler!"

Städtische Kunstgewerbeschule Frankfurt am Main

Frankfurt am Main, 16. Dezember 1933.

In der Anlage erhalten Sie eine Bestätigung über die Dauer Ihres Besuches unserer Anstalt. Ein Zeugnis können wir im Hinblick auf die Gründe, die zu Ihrer Ausscheidung führten, nicht erteilen.

Heil Hitler !

Herrn
Munie Weinraub
Zürich
St. Annagasse 17

Letter informing Munio Weinraub that the Frankfurt School of Art cannot provide a certificate of the duration of his studies due to the reasons for his exclusion (1933). Personal archives of Amos Gitai

Between 1931, the date of the first letter, and 1933, things changed very quickly. The form expresses meaning very directly; these letters illustrate this. Architecture, too, is always a political gesture. These three letters, each with a one-year gap, testify to rapid political change.
Returning to cinema: today, artisanal cinema has become rarer because financiers don't like it. They want to know immediately, in advance, what the final film will be like because it's easier for budgeting. But the cinema I defend is a continuous dialogue. To reference my culture, it is a Talmudic approach of interpretation and reinterpretation, right up to the very end. The cinema I love is the one that adopts the approach I've outlined regarding architecture. The text explains what needs to be communicated to others, what the project will be. But it's not yet the film, even if it's well-written. Now we have to decide how to shoot, what the rhythm is, how to choreograph each scene, how to integrate elements that don't depend on us, like weather conditions, chance. How to remain sensitive, attentive, how to integrate chance, give it shape? Integrating chance into artistic work is something that cinema no longer recognizes. Financiers want the script executed. But a certain type of cinema, very much in the minority, still retains this artisanal aspect, which I believe is necessary.

Obsessions

33 theses

Stefano Boeri

A few weeks ago, a dear Italian friend, Silvia Brena, a journalist and writer, asked me to summarize my perception of the "state of things" in a few sentences; in other words, she asked me to try to synthesize my perspective on contemporary world events. It was an almost impossible request, but I found it amusing to try. I began by reminding Silvia of the books by Donna Haraway, an ethologist, zoologist, and philosopher who speaks of the *Chthulucene*, the era that should replace the Anthropocene. For Haraway, the *Chthulucene* is "a salvific era that will lead us out of a catastrophic period dominated by humans, towards a cultural model aimed at generating kinship in a very broad sense . . ."
Haraway also talks about re-establishing our relationship with other living species in a new form of cohabitation and cooperation.
But it is worth carefully considering the concepts, which are very popular today, of "overcoming the Anthropocene" and the Post-Human.
Here are some of the points drawn from the 45 theses (or rather hypotheses), published by Silvia in the book *Parole in Tempesta: Dizionario della Contemporaneità* (2024, Il Saggiatore), which she sent me after our conversation:

1. The theme of the Anthropocene and its centrality is misplaced. Exiting the Anthropocene is itself a paradox: we cannot resign from our role as a thinking species. The only way to think about exiting the Anthropocene is our extinction. I don't think that is in the realm of possibility, nor desirable.

2. We have an obligation, as a species, to produce a holistic vision of the world and the sphere of the living. Thinking of overcoming the Anthropocene makes no sense; it means abdicating our role as the hegemonic species.

opposite page
Stefano Boeri Architetti, Master plan for a Smart Forest City, Cancún, Mexico, 2019

3. As the dominant species, we have a responsibility towards other living beings: to create conditions for greater equity, encompassing more exchanges and interactions among the species that populate the planet.

4. We need to focus on two words, in the present and for the future: connection and biodiversity.
These prelude the possibility of building systems capable of relating and interacting, even at a distance, between different environments and territories.

5. Connect, from the Latin *nectere*, to weave, to join. We must create biodiversity corridors that connect different places. We are doing this with the Parco Italia project.
We aim to link nature reserves, national parks, marine parks, and regional parks.

6. Connections must be experienced. The green corridors we are creating with Parco Italia will also become practicable routes.

7. Connections help to multiply the positive effects that biodiversity systems have in enhancing the cohabitation of living species.

8. The future model is no longer the network.

9. The network, as a mere connection of fixed points, no longer works. Today we are moving toward the meshwork, a term coined by British anthropologist Tim Ingold.

10. The network, which has shaped the contemporary era, including technologically (world wide web), operates on the connection of fixed identities. The future speaks instead of a web of flows, of identities in motion.

11. Identity is a journey, a constant movement. It is not stable. After all, nothing in nature is stable, starting with subatomic particles.

12. The network is not a network but a web that is continually redesigned between subjects in motion: in their bodies, their environments, their minds.

13. The web arises from connections. Interaction creates the flow, designs it, and gives it form. We are what we are because of the interactions we produce.

14. The web of flows is the only way to face the challenge of artificial intelligence.

15. We live in a constant state of intentional transition. And, as philosopher Paul B. Preciado teaches, this journey can also be experienced by individuals, who can reject biological determinism in defining their gender.

16. In this sense, mutation is a constructive project. Why stop at simple identity coding? Today I am male, but I can try to explore.

17. Continuous mutation inevitably impacts the housing models we are designing. It translates first of all into a new concept of family. The family must be understood as a project, not as a predefined code of exclusion (who is in and who is out, based on identity).

18. The family is a housing project that stabilizes in relation to a space.

19. Today, the tripartition of living, working, and leisure time is broken. The horizons of biopolitics are now defined by the design of spaces.

20. The real issue is the concept of nature, the living nature that must be brought back into the urban condition.

21. Living nature is not an ornament. Nor is it reducible to a compromise between built space and green space. It is a constitutive element of the human habitat.

22. Not only are we part of nature, but nature must become part of our living space again.

23. For this reason, we have been working on this theme for twenty years, somewhat obsessively. We started working on forestry, then on vertical forests, and now we are working on biodiversity connections and corridors.

24. One must be obsessive to be incisive. It means establishing a line of coherence and rigour for oneself and one's work. If cultivated, especially professionally, obsession, much more than passion, can be a great resource.

25. We are nature. The dualism must be overcome.

26. As nature, we are finite beings.

27. Fluidity and transformation, however, imply a different relationship with the finitude that we are. Think of cocoon coffins that are then germinated and our body becomes compost. Thus, we become a tree.

28. Life is the opening of a perspective on the world that then at some point closes and ends there. I say this, lucidly and desperately, as an atheist.

29. There is no doubt that we should facilitate a form of conversion of organic matter, capable of transforming into something else and re-entering the life cycle.

30. Today we must also think about the end of life of buildings. When buildings are constructed, they should always incorporate an idea of their finitude. Meaning how materials are used, how they will be recycled and recovered.

31. Finitude is a beautiful word and a driver of innovation.

32. A negative, penitential narrative of climate change must be avoided:

Stefano Boeri Architetti, Master plan for the Ramagrama Stupa, Lumbini, Nepal, 2023

a sacrificial representation in which to do less harm, to be sustainable, we must renounce, renounce, and renounce.

33. Climate change is instead a great opportunity. There is a convergence of environmental and health benefits: improving our diet, the way we move around the city, our relationship with nature is a way of improving our quality of life, as well as reducing our environmental impact.

Perception

How I see the world

Stefano Boeri

I am color-blind, affected since birth by red-green color vision deficiency, or more precisely, deuteranopia. Specifically, I struggle to distinguish between green and brown.
In essence, while I can perceive the differences and nuances in the wide range of objects, spaces, animals, and plants that we define as green or brown, I struggle to discern the boundary line between these two fields. It's as if, instead of a clear line in the color palette, there is a large blurred patch that, in lighter tones, resembles a vast beige. As if that weren't enough, I confess that I also have some difficulty distinguishing between blue and purple. (Recently, I mistook the purple background of a weather forecast indicating a stormy sea as a calm sea, putting my small fishing boat at risk in the midst of the waves; image on page 221.)
If colors were nations, instead of borders, my geopolitics would see a vast free zone or an extensive transnational conurbation. If they were languages, in some areas I would hear their voices replaced by powerful dialects like Ladino, or like the *grammelot* of Dario Fo.
But these are imprecise explanations, simply because I don't know how others see; I don't know how you see. I simply suppose.
My older brother, with whom I share the same "defect," along with an uncle who is color-blind on my mother's side (deuteranopia is determined by genes located on the X chromosome, which is only present in duplicate in females), helped me, as a child, not to pay attention to the teasing at school about my drawings of brown meadows and greenish horses.
The first slight shock came at the age of 16, during the exam for the motorcycle license, when a doctor of few words told me that I would "never be able to drive a Formula 1 car or an airplane," but also that—as a con-

opposite page
top: Boeri Studio, Bosco Verticale, Milan, Italy, 2014
bottom: Visual representation of the Bosco Verticale with a deuteranopia filter

solation—"the US Air Force was using soldiers who were deuteranopic like me to spot (yes . . . we see shades better) Viet Cong positions camouflaged in the jungle." Oh well . . .

The truth is that over the years I developed a sort of obsession precisely with that part of the world and for those phenomena that—according to the standards of "normal" color perception—belong to the realm of green and brown. It is therefore an obsession with a dark area: with what I saw but couldn't classify.

My "problem" is essentially one of communication: we lack the words to name what we see (in the European population, about eight percent of males and one percent of females are affected by partial color blindness; in Italy, one in twelve men and one in twenty women are considered "sufferers" of this visual impairment), since the common vocabulary related to colors defines chromatic classes that we simply do not recognize.

And so, without realizing it, over the course of my life, the rich beige of the natural world, so vibrant with nuances, gradually overlapped the white, black, and gray of my Milanese childhood and adolescence (and even my early architectural works like the RCS tower, endowed with a rather dull play of variations on gray). I began to pose a simple and basic question: was I seeing a different reality, or was I seeing the same reality differently?

Witnessing, as a preadolescent, the divorce between a neurologist father passionate about inventive processes and an architect mother with an implacable sensitivity to colors certainly did not help me choose between a restless relativistic position and a serenely materialistic one.

Today, I perceive my color blindness, mild or not, as the awareness of a condition common to our species (the plasticity of our Homo sapiens brain) and, at the same time, I confess, as a small but unmistakable confirmation of the loneliness of human existence.

As with tinnitus, which I am familiar with, or taste distortions (I experienced them during my Covid convalescence), deuteranopia seems to be the result of non-canonical activity of neuronal networks. These networks, unable to correct an imperfection (the absence of a visual pig-

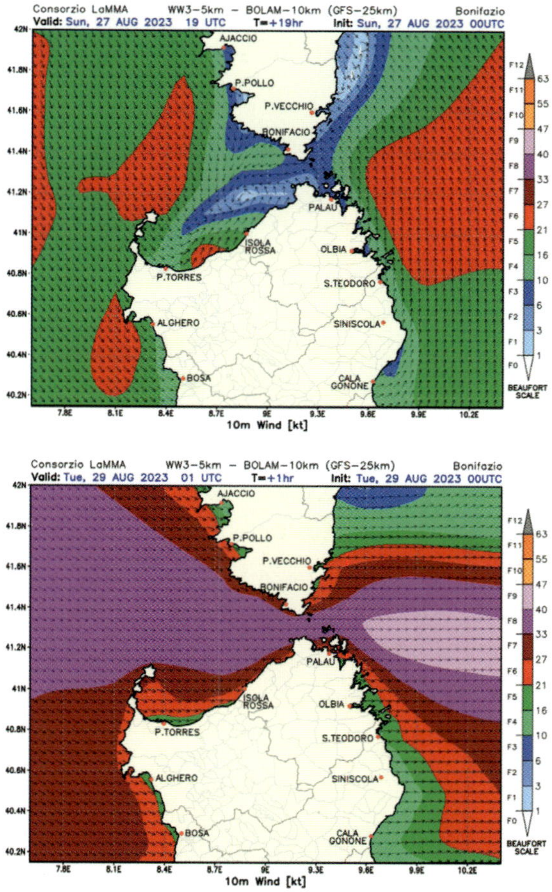

Forecasts of the average wind at ten meters above sea level for August 27 and 29, 2023

ment in the retina), provide an anomalous response, namely one that does not conform to the norm.

The malfunctioning of a protein, opsins, in our optic cone is reshaped by our very own brain synapses to the point of determining a perception of color that varies from individual to individual—so different that it cannot even be shared with those who have my same type of color blindness. That immense and vibrant beige, which for me—and perhaps for a few others—contains a part of the chromatic reality of the world, is therefore nothing but confirmation that despite daily efforts to fill it with affection and interactions, to color it with shared tones, our lives remain a solitary construction; never colorless, but irretrievably individual.

Munio's Homage

Lullaby to my father Munio Gitai Weinraub (1909-1970)

Amos Gitai

Munio, my father,
Like the people of his generation
Applied to his architecture
A dimension of modesty, of restraint
Of submission to the collective project.
And this is also part of the tradition of the Bauhaus
Not only orthogonal buildings.

Let's say I wanted to develop a film project
That draws on his biography
And also on geography
And on architectural geometry
I would try to interweave the movements
The historical and political ones
Which created and shaped
The minimalist language, the factual one
These are consequences of the rationalization of design
And the technological revolution
That every city like Berlin went through
By the beginning of the twentieth century
The period we are dealing with
Berlin, a kind of a Prussian agglomerate of townlets
Which needed a unifying style
Of an industrial rationale
As well as the beginning of the thought of
Habitation for the masses
In the context of mass culture

opposite page
Munio Weinraub Gitai at the Bauhaus, Dessau, Germany, 1929

Like the one of Benjamin, Adorno, Marcuse
In another city, Frankfurt, but at the same period
The creation of a theory
And its architectural iconography
In the architectural language it's called Hilberseimer and Hannes Meyer.
The latter, together with Walter Gropius
Sent Munio, who was eighteen years old
And had just arrived from the Silesian-Polish-German town
Of Bielsko-Biała or Bilitz—
Like in our places it depends on who counts the territory
The Polish, the Germans, or the Austro-Hungarians—
And then Hannes Meyer met the young Munio
And recommended to him that before he is admitted to the Bauhaus
In Dessau, he should learn carpentry in a school of neoclassical style
The Tischlerschule
Meaning the opposed design ideology
Out of recognition that these "reactionary conservatives"
Know how to use wood.

And after a year of professionalizing himself in
Neoclassical ornaments
Munio was admitted to the Bauhaus
And there, according to the best of dialectics they implemented
His technological know-how of wood
While challenging the design.

The film will ask therefore questions of macro:
How did the young Munio move
From Bilitz, through Dessau, to the atelier of the last legendary
Director of the Bauhaus Mies van der Rohe?
And how did he work on the last exhibit before Hitler
In nineteen thirty-one?
And how were Jews and socialists chased away from the Bauhaus at a period
When Mies van der Rohe

Thought that he could appease the Nazis
By firing and chasing some of the students
The radicals, or the Jews, or the Jewish radicals
And how did it happen that he did not succeed
I mean Mies van der Rohe
And that the Nazis did not accept his proposition to design their party's
Central Office in Munich?
So Munio was saved for History's sake
By the Nazi's bad, Kitsch and monumental taste.

As for Munio
He was arrested and beaten and his teeth were broken.
And was released by the father of his non-Jewish lover
Smuggled by his friends to the border
Of Switzerland
To Basel
Where Herzl had held his first Zionist Congress.

But this was before, in eighteen ninety-seven.
There, in Basel, Herzl spoke
About the creation of a *Judenstadt*, a Jewish state
Modern and secular
And fantasized about Haifa as a big port city
Without rabbis and military officers
But an industrial capital
A modern city
Like the one that Munio would try to design
Forty years later
After he had escaped from Europe on a deck of a boat
Roughly at the period when the Swiss started to return the
German Jews to Germany.
And he thought that this was a good time to go East
And try something different.
Building industry in the Haifa Bay

That of Herzl
And also designing kibbutzim
And children's rooms for the collective education
For those who wanted to create a new human being
Almost social realism.
And also to design mass public housing for those
Who would soon escape Europe as well as North Africa.

Munio is standing with a hat
With a simple suit and tie in a color which fits
The color of the suit in the heat of Eretz Israel
Like an immigrant.

It is clear that he comes from somewhere else, and
He gives a lecture. To whom?
To construction workers, telling them of the principles
Of modernism and about brick as a basic module.
Then he travels in Emeq Israel, and the Jordan valley
To design collective dining rooms for the kibbutzim of Hashomer Hatzair.

The kibbutzniks, who in many domains were innovative
And courageous
Were very conservative in their architectural taste.
They don't like the orthogonal architecture
With the flat roofs
Somehow, it reminds them of Arab villages
And this is obviously something much more inferior.
They prefer the pastoral image
Of little townlets and shtetls with tiled red roofs.

How will the audacious architect act in such a revolutionary
Conservative context? An enigma.
But Munio and his friends succeeded partially
And that's why the architectural iconography of this period

Is modern
They engraved and shaped in the collective memory.
The matter-of-fact simplicity of a design without ornaments
Unlike the one which is current now in our places
Shared by men, women, and children alike
That a Jewish building needs a kippa on its head
Who at all said that a kippa or a dome is a Jewish motif?
But today, certainly in Jerusalem
There are more and more domes and kippas, in more
Than in one sense.

And in nineteen forty-eight the State of Israel is created
A big event which shapes new frontiers
Also of our consciousness.
And also many Palestinian refugees
But this is another matter which continues
And should continue to occupy us today.

The new state creates a Ministry of Housing headed
By Golda Meir
Who nominates Munio to be the head of the
Architectural department of the new state
Although she reprimands him for not being
A Party member.
That was the practice
And in many places this is still the habit today.
But Munio and the people of his generation succeeded to outline
The urban and architectural criteria of the new state.
This is also the time to design Yad Vashem
And the Hebrew University in Givat Ram in Jerusalem
And design the passenger ships
That Israel gets as a partial compensation from Germany
And the site of the government in Jerusalem
In the same year in which I was born.

Not all the projects would be realized
And most of the buildings of this period
Would not be conserved.
This activity would continue until nineteen sixty-seven
A year that we think lasted only six days
Because this is the name of the war which erupted in June
In the center of the year.

So let's rewind and go back to seven years earlier.
In this year Munio created his office anew
And in the good old tradition he decides once more
To design a dining room for a kibbutz
Kfar Masaryk.
The same kibbutz where ten years later
Meaning nineteen seventy
On the 24th of the month of September
He will die and be buried
In Kfar Masaryk

The cemetery is placed in the fields
Open to the horizon
Somehow again a repeat of an almost social realist image
Of the Herzl dream of a Jew cultivating his land
And dying there.

So in nineteen sixty Munio goes to Kfar Masaryk
Somehow tired and sick of the years that passed
And he takes upon himself the challenge
To give form and shape to this original invention of the kibbutz
The dining room.

Original, since the kibbutz wanted to replace religion
With another form of community
So the dining room, not the synagogue, is there to install a daily routine

After all, people have to eat several times a day
It is the meeting place for the committees of the kibbutz who will run all the affairs of the collective.
It is the place for celebrations, the holiday feasts, the theater performances, and the cinema screenings
It is also the place to put the mailboxes of each member
So by its multifunctional character par excellence
This building presents a challenge to the architect.

Munio chooses a modern architectural language, not a sentimental one.
The space will be divided by three patios
And its main hall will face the kibbutz landscape.
In some way, by its simplicity, minimalism, and rigueur
This will be one of the highlights of his work.

The construction of the building will start in nineteen sixty-three and last for almost four years.
The building will be completed by nineteen sixty-seven
Now Munio is left with only three years to live.
They discovered a rare blood cancer, a form of leukemia
Now he decides to Hebraize his name to Gitai
From the root *gat* press
And the conjugation of *banai*, builder
Meaning the worker who will take grapes to the wine press
And make out of them wine
Or the worker who will take olives to the olive press
To produce pure olive oil.
It is of course a process in which there is squeezing
Either of the olive or the grape
So they will become pure,
Unique and distilled liquid.

But in this year the face of Israeli architecture is changing as well
Following the new empire that was just conquered
The Israeli architects adopt
A style that the British call
And this is really the technical term
Brutal architecture
And then crusader-like citadels are being erected in the West Bank
Brutal architecture with narrow, cracked windows and bare armed concrete
The bon ton of this period is also that of contempt for the
Fragile minimalist architecture
Of the previous generation.

The Angel of Death liberates Munio from his sufferings
And also from the need to collaborate—yes, to collaborate
With a new aggressive architecture.

Signed:
His young son, Amos

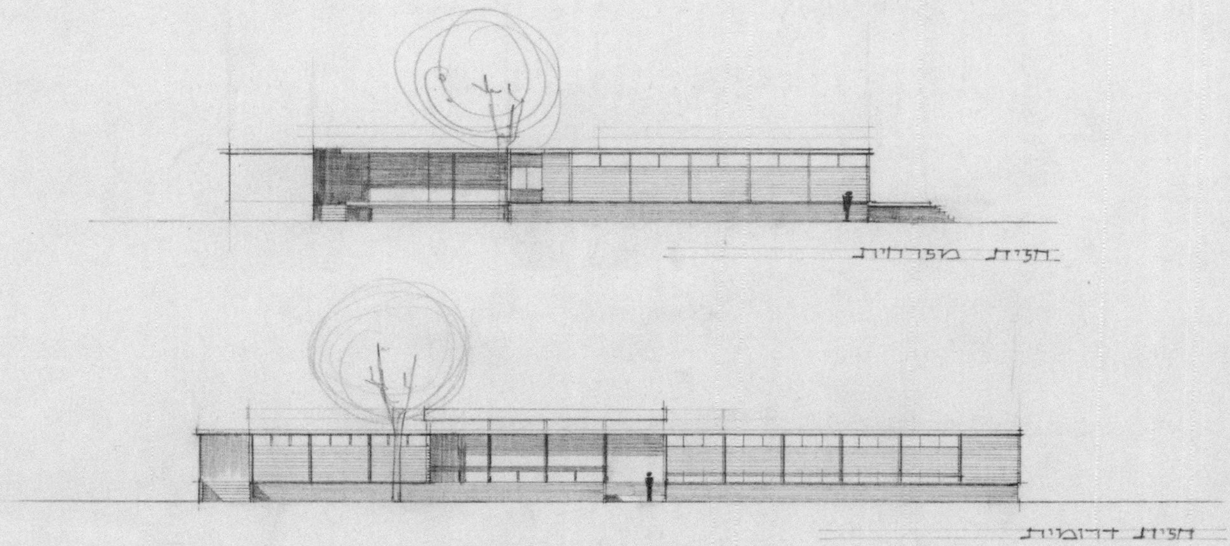

Sketch for the dining room of kibbutz Kfar Masaryk by Munio Weinraub Gitai, 1963

Kibbutz Kfar Masaryk, Dining hall courtyard designed by Munio Weinraub Gitai.
Photo by Gabriele Basilico, 1992

Renato Boeri (1922–1994), 1992

Renato
My father
Stefano Boeri

My father, Renato Boeri, was a neurologist with an abiding focus on neuropsychology studies.
His reflections on brain synapses and the interdependencies between physiology and the cognitive reactivity of the human brain stimulated me to observe the territory and the city as a field, analogous to actions and retroactions that weave together the matter of space, human behaviors and the collective imagination.
Indeed, like the gigantic orchestra of neurons that is the human brain, the territory is never subdivisible into separate sections, not least because its housing practices sometimes create effects at a great distance.
There are no watertight compartments in urban phenomena.
Every departure of functions and life from an urban center causes the opening of large voids in the compact body of the city—as if it were an inevitable stretch mark—right where the same lives were previously concentrated. On the other hand, the urbanization of large portions of the population historically corresponds to the emptying and abandonment of rural villages, historic hamlets, and the countryside.
The physical morphology and the social morphology of the city cannot be conceived, thought of, or studied independently. Every act of extension of human life in one place often corresponds to a parallel process of retraction of dwelling and social emptying of another, precisely because the energies manifested in this tensioning of spaces by human society are not infinite.

Human behaviors not only flow over spaces, encountering varying degrees of friction, but also shape them. In other words, when we look at a territory, along with its physical geography, we must consider the changing behavior of its inhabitants in space, two spheres that continually intersect and condition each other.

Likewise, we must look at the evolution of the urban condition over time. A city is the outcome of a temporal stratification that leaves traces that—no matter how much they may be eroded or obliterated—remain in the present of urban life, conditioning its future.

An architectural historian like André Corboz used to say that the contemporary city is a *palimpsest*. It is a wrinkled surface, created by the superimposition of the legacies of different epochs of human life, on which transitions between different cultures and styles of living are continually activated and deposited, and become new physical and social landscapes, which in turn will leave traces and ruins on which new places and new vital relationships can arise. For this reason, the evolution of a city must be observed both by considering its nature as a palimpsest and by paying attention to the expectations of the communities that inhabit it today. This means observing the effects that the spaces and buildings inherited from history have and will have on their behavior and needs.

The city and the inhabited area are thus a vital and changing palimpsest. In addition to the legacies of the past, they also bear the traces of a series of transitional states that reflect the more or less intense presence of our species and the use we make, today, of the space we inhabit.

Cini

My mother

Stefano Boeri

At home, when I was a child, she had a white table, one of those ones with squares. She used to design there, in front of the window, looking at the bell tower of the Basilica of Sant'Ambrogio, where she was born. She never stopped. Until the end, until a few hours before she died, she drew with her hands. She measured spaces, the height of people, the distances . . .
Cini Boeri, my mother, was an architect.
On the construction site, she was very authoritative, extremely determined—the only woman in a world of men, whose initial skepticism she had to overcome. But she was also very open and curious; she liked talking to the masons, and often found solutions together with them.

Cini loved to go to La Maddalena, in Sardinia, where in 1967 she had built a small concrete house nestled on the granite rocks, just a few meters from the sea. Cini adored the wind that often sweeps through the Strait of Bonifacio and its archipelagos. I only saw her truly happy there, on certain days of wild Mistral, when for everyone else it was impossible even to take a swim. The more extreme the wind was, the happier she was.

Maria Cristina Mariani Dameno, known to everyone throughout her life simply as Cini (from the Lombard "*picinin*," the littlest of three siblings) Boeri (the surname of my father Renato, a neurologist whom she met during the Resistance, when she a partisan courier and he was the commander of a partisan brigade), was my mother. But above all, she was one of the architects and designers who best and most foresightedly captured her time and anticipated ours. With absolute autonomy. Because autonomy is the key to understanding her way of designing. And living. Which have always been one and the same.

To understand it, we must start from La Maddalena, and from that "bunker house," as the locals called it, almost a monolith landed on the cliffs overlooking the sea, which Cini shaped for our family. A "tent," she called it, "that fostered the happiest days, with absolute autonomy and simultaneously with the joy of being together."
It was 1967; I was 11 years old and on the construction site I took photos of her and my brothers, Tito and Sandro. The house was designed and built just before my parents' divorce, and I have always thought that the choice of two separate rooms for them was a way to avoid what eventually happened.
So that self-imposed model of coexistence didn't work, but her idea was already emerging clearly: a large central space for socializing and four nuclei, effectively studio apartments, each with independent access to the sea, for her, her husband, the children, and friends.

When in 1986, Cini theorized this vision at the Triennale in the exhibition *Domestic Project*—a house for young couples with rooms for dreaming and loving, for individual reflection and creative dialogue—she was even accused of being a "marriage killer." The same marriages that, she argued, should last for five years and then, if necessary, be reconfirmed: by choice, not obligation.

Moreover, reflection on couples has always been central for Cini, even in her architecture. She was convinced that love needed freedom, and this was reflected in the spaces. Autonomy, for her, was not a dilution of emotional energies or distancing, but rather the right distance that allowed you to be together more and more intensely. Always with responsibility. Hers was a radical feminism, but without rhetoric or ideology, applied to life.

The house in Sardinia also embodies a second distinctive trait of my mother: elegance. Hers was an elegance that was never elitist or born out of self-satisfaction, however. It was an ethical elegance, rational, linked to profound simplicity. She loved the style of Armani, the dance of Pina Bausch, and the cinema of Joseph Losey, a highly sophisticated yet dry, linear director.

These three figures give an idea of her cultural and visual universe. And of her design objects, like the family of Strips, which certainly had great success and encapsulated Cini's democratic sense of design well. I adore the sofas of the *Bobo* series and the *Serpentone*, a visionary and intelligent project, which were never mass-produced because the technology at the time could not support all the performance aspects she demanded from this infinite seating system, but with a beautiful, flexible yet essential section.

I worked with my mother only once, on a project for a villa near Basel. It was the meeting of two different ways of thinking about architecture: I tended to focus on the external shell; she started from the interiors and the movement of people within the spaces. It resulted in a kind of hybrid, which was not particularly successful.

In Sardinia, in the 1970s Cini had designed the setup of the Casa-Museo of Antonio Gramsci in Ghilarza, the birthplace of the founder of the Italian Communist Party, imprisoned by Mussolini and left to die behind bars. Unfortunately, the municipal administration of Ghilarza has almost erased that project, but it is an absolute masterpiece. And it also tells of her political passion. Throughout her life, she was a communist, without any doubt.

Thanks to her acquaintance with Vando Aldrovandi, known as Al, a partisan commander of the Garibaldi Brigade, brother-in-law of Giulio Einaudi and a highly cultured bookseller, a mediator between the leaders of the PCI and the intellectual bourgeoisie of Milan, everyone passed through our house: Amendola, Napolitano, even Berlinguer . . . And I remember that we, the children, who sympathized with the movements to the left of the PCI, looked with some annoyance at this "occupation" of the Communist Party in our home.

She often said, "designing joy," which for her meant injecting irony into her work, but above all, thinking about the happiness of those who inhabited her spaces.

She had an obsession with everything that was visually beautiful. If she considered something or someone "ugly," there was nothing to be done about it. And then there were the colors: the pink of the carpet in the apartment in Sant'Ambrogio, the beige, the blue.
She was always on the move, both physically and intellectually. One evening, I accompanied her to a dinner at Vittorio Gregotti's. I still remember Gae Aulenti's unforgettable voice from the terrace: "Cini, you are relentless."

During the most difficult period after the separation, she took us to Paris. Only it was May 1968, the city was burning, and we ended up on the barricades, amidst the occupied Sorbonne. I don't know where she found it, but she bought a used Daimler, a convertible with which we toured Milan.
And I remember that in 1967, together with Al, she decided to join the protests against the colonels' coup in Greece. I don't know how, but we managed to break through the police cordon outside the consulate, and once inside, in front of the Consul, she had us pull out the signs she had hidden under our golf shirts: "Colonels murderers!" Unbelievable . . . she was like that. Like the wind she loved.

previous pages
Cini Boeri, Casa Bunker,
La Maddalena, Sardinia,
Italy, 1967

Cini Boeri (1924–2020), Milan, Italy, 1972

Natalie Portman in *Free Zone* (2005)

Against Interpretation

Rhythm, beauty, and imperfection as creative parameters

Amos Gitai

Free Zone is a film I did in 2005. It's a story that was told to me by a guy who works as a driver for the film industry in Israel, and at some point in his life he was unemployed. We always have major disputes because he used to speak about the Arabs in a condescending manner, but when he explained to me what he was doing in order to overcome his economic difficulties, I was very surprised. Since he couldn't find work in Israel, he would bring 4x4 cars from Houston, Texas, to his workshop in an agricultural village in the desert, and he would transform these cars into armored vehicles, then cross the border to Jordan and, together with his Palestinian partner, sell them to US security companies in Iraq. After he told me the story, I decided to embark on the journey with him; we went to this *Free Zone* in Jordan where buyers and sellers coming from the entire Middle East go in order to do business. I saw Tel Aviv buses with tickers "Vote Sharon" written in Hebrew next to Saudi Arabia businessmen . . . It was surreal! When I returned from this trip, I decided to transform the three male characters into female characters: the Israeli driver became Hana Laszlo, who received Best Actress Award at the 2005 Cannes film festival for this role, his Palestinian partner the great Palestinian actress Hiam Abbass, and me, the passenger, became someone much more beautiful . . . Natalie Portman.

When I showed the film at the Serpentine Gallery in London, the architect Pierre de Meuron had an interesting comment. He said to me: "The fragment of your film Free Zone is impressive because somehow *it doesn't need interpretation.* It would even destroy its strength. . . . This amazing face of Natalie Portman crying is like a sculpture. . . . The window goes up and down and this gesture becomes very architectural. The sound comes

in and is again closing and it goes away. So, the sound is not just the sound but it carries a kind of cultural information: this is about Arabic, Jewish and Christian architectural monuments. In this fragment there are so many ingredients of what makes our lives interesting but also difficult and then this music makes it so rich, and at the same time it opens doors to architecture and to so many issues that we might share or explore together . . . Doing a film about architecture is extremely hard. I have not even seen one which is not boring. This is why I like the way you situate that figure in a space so it's not just a figure, not just a narrative or an argument, but this space becomes meaningful as a form of *interpretation*."
There are many parallels that unite architecture and cinema. Both mediums are non-intimate arts that require some talent to bring together people from different origins, to give them a common sense of mission, so that the outcome will be a great building or film. Both start with a text, be it a program for a new construction or a screenplay for a film. But the text doesn't have a physical shape, we have to translate this verbal expression into form. It reminds me of the Golem (I can still hear the voice of Jorge Luis Borges reading his poem "El Golem"), this very fist artefact, which was later taken by the expressionists to install the idea of the potential hopes and the risks/dangers of objects created by humans. They can help "progress" but they can also be destructive. This leads us to discuss the issues of beauty and aesthetics in the creation of forms. Also, one of the great dilemmas of the present is the following: How will the advanced digital tools of design help or cripple the architectural "product"? (I use the term "product" since sometimes we feel that these architectural creatures have been pre-simulated in a mechanical Golem-like manner.) Cinema and architecture both need technological know-how so that they can become erected into reality. And both disciplines require a good and enlightened commissioner, one who will reach to the ambitions of excellence, and a humanly acceptable materialization of the idea, be it the producer of a film or the person who orders a new building from the architect. Let's hope for the best.
One thing really stayed with me from my years at Berkeley. In Christopher Alexander's class, we spent a semester trying to define beauty. It's

almost impossible to do, but we had ten rugs from Alexander's personal collection, and we were supposed to decide which one was the most beautiful, based on its formal characteristics, symmetry, colors, etc. We usually chose the one that had a small flaw, and looking back, I think it's because it broke the perfection. And this is where beauty is to be found. Sometimes, we may be able to understand beauty, but that doesn't mean we can reproduce it. It's like many things in life. We can understand certain things; it doesn't mean that we can immediately create a manual to start producing beautiful things. We should privilege understatement.

Collective Housing

Ionesco's *Rhinoceros* as a Shikun, a call for action

Amos Gitai

Inspired by Eugène Ionesco's play, my film Shikun recounts the emergence of intolerance and totalitarian thinking through a series of day-to-day episodes that take place in Israel in a single building, the Shikun. In this hybrid group of people of different origins and languages, some turn into rhinoceroses, but others resist. This is an ironic metaphor for life in our contemporary societies.

Shikun in Hebrew means "social housing," a building for people to live in. The word comes from a verb meaning "to shelter," "to give refuge." And the film gives shelter to people who, for different reasons, need refuge from the threat of rhinos. I like the sound of the word, I know that most people won't know what it means, but that doesn't bother me, on the contrary. There's something abstract about it that suits me, that's in the spirit of the project.

The film was born in relation to what was then the context in Israel, before October 7. We were in the middle of a huge protest movement against the attempt by Netanyahu and his far-right government to reform the legal system, with large demonstrations bringing together feminist groups, soldiers, academics, economists, people campaigning for peaceful coexistence between Palestinians and Israelis and a large section of civil society against the destruction of the democratic legal system. This movement was also a reaction to the rise of a form of conformism, the disappearance of critical thinking in Israeli society. It was in this context that I reread Ionesco's play *Rhinoceros*, written at the end of the 1950s as an anti-totalitarian fable, which seemed to me to echo what we were experiencing. I saw in it the possibility of inspiration for a film about the present we were living in. At the time, I was in Tel Aviv rehearsing the stage version of *House*, a play inspired by my 1980 film. The whole cast was there, including Irène Jacob and the Palestinian actress Bahira Ablassi. At the same time as we were working on the play, we got collectively involved in this project, which I wrote quite quickly. I called the cinematographer Eric Gautier, with whom I've worked on four of my previous films over the last twelve years, and he arrived straight away. We were able to put together the material conditions and shoot without delay, thanks also to the complicity of the producers, technicians, and artists with whom I have this long relationship of collaboration and friendship.

The first part of the film was entirely scripted for this particular building, whose architecture helped me to structure the story, to organize the way we see the cohabitation and interference of the very different people who live there. It creates a spatial unit in which Israelis, Palestinians, Ukrainians, and so on move around. All these people belong to everyday reality, and among them is a special person, played by Irène Jacob, who is frightened by the emergence of these creatures, the rhinoceroses.

The shikun is a well-known building, said to be the longest in the Middle East, stretching over 250 meters. And it's indeed a shikun, a social housing building. It stands in the town of Beer-Sheva, in the center of the Negev desert in southern Israel. The building itself is a powerful architectural gesture, in the spirit of Le Corbusier, a kind of *coup de force*, a statement in the middle of the desert. Its spatial organization, perspectives, angles, and building materials helped me to bring these different characters and activities to life in contiguous ways, which can be conflicting or simply ignore each other, without having to create artificial sequences, series of causes and effects, as too many films force themselves to do.

The film is about the chaos of the world, the chaos created by war, economic inequality, and injustice. Most films tend to soften this chaos by assembling logical, psychological, sociological, and other explanations for behavior, which reassures the audience. But in my view this is a delusion. Reality is the result of heterogeneous forces, chance, and illogical interference. And in the midst of all this, there is an active force: fear. Fear is not a given, it's constructed, it's manufactured, and leaders like

Parcours exhibition designed by Amos Gitai in an abandoned submarine base from World War II, Evento Biennial, Bordeaux, France, 2009

Trump, Netanyahu, Orban, Putin, etc. are engineers of fear, and obviously so is Hamas. They thrive on the feeling of fear that they produce and maintain. This is what rhinos represent metaphorically, and this is what we must resist.

Shikun belongs to a group of films I've made recently that are characterized by what I could call a semi-enclosed camera: *Laila in Haifa* (2020), *A Tramway in Jerusalem* (2018), *Ana Arabia* (2013), or even going back to *Alila* (2003). They are all set entirely within a delimited space, but with glimpses of the outside world in one way or another. Each time the project is to explore a microcosm with the ambition that it will reflect a more general truth, in much the same way as the study of a cell would provide a representation of, and information about, an entire living body. This unity of place, and indeed also of time, implies some fairly radical formal choices, which organize the flow of movement and make the forces that concentrate and oppose each other visible. One of these directorial choices is clearly the use of the sequence shot—which I took to extremes for *Ana Arabia*, which is entirely filmed in a single shot. But the precise answers are different each time; the sequence shots in *Shikun* are not the same as in my other films, and neither is the editing.

The film's aim is not to provide ready-made answers, but to open up questions, provoke confusion, and encourage viewers to make their own way. And neither the actors nor I know all the reasons for what's going on; it's a search for each and every one of us, a kind of quest. At best, we understand what we've done after we've done it. When you have sequence shots with a large number of moving protagonists and complex camera movements, you cannot improvise; you have to adjust everything to the millimeter. The film is born of this requirement, as well as of the openness of our questioning.

The dialogues are in several languages, including Hebrew and Arabic. For those who don't speak these languages, it can be difficult to know which one is being used. But this is deliberate, and I didn't want the subtitles to help differentiate them, for example by using two colors as is often done. This obviously creates an asymmetry between those who know these languages and those who don't, which is also interesting. The fact that there's uncertainty for people who don't come from this region, who don't speak the languages, is part of the film's proposition. Above all, I don't want to be didactic.

Although the central literary reference is Ionesco, the film also draws on other literary sources. It ends with a poem by Mahmoud Darwish, "Think of Others," and includes a passage from Umberto Eco on cowardice and a text by Israeli journalist and writer Amira Hass, who was the Haaretz newspaper's correspondent in the occupied territories, Gaza and the West Bank, for decades. I believe she's still in Ramallah. In the film, the line "Our children will ask: how could you [inflict the injustices and atrocities inflicted on the Palestinians for so many years]?" is based on one of her writings.

The film was conceived and made prior to October 7, before the Hamas terrorist attacks and the Israeli army's war to destroy Gaza. Inevitably, these atrocious events resonate with the film. After October 7 and what followed, I hesitated, I wondered what to do, I considered not releasing the film, or modifying it. In the end I decided to show it exactly as it was made. It seems to me that the film is internally coherent, and that what is shown in it can also be shared in today's context. Perhaps, given the proliferation of rhinoceroses, it offers an even more relevant approach.

The ferocity of Hamas's actions, the destruction of kibbutzim, the murder of civilians, the killing of young people dancing at a concert, the acts of barbarism, and the rape of women are atrocious acts. They are not only anti-Israeli, they are also anti-Palestinian, because they destroy the option of dialogue between the two peoples. The only possible perspective. I listen to the speeches of those who put everything together, creating confusion in this tragedy . . . But even a national resistance doesn't justify this type of barbarism and violence. Burning people alive, killing children in front of their parents . . . Nothing justifies such actions. It will postpone the necessary agreement between Israelis and Palestinians, because it's clear that a workable *modus vivendi* must be found between the two peoples. There is no other option.

The current vicious cycle makes one want to cry. Netanyahu's government is made up of fundamentalists, members of the far right, racists, who carry out provocations in Jerusalem, on the Mount of Olives. For months, before October 7, hundreds of thousands of Israelis demonstrated against this government every week. The feeling today is similar to that of fifty years ago. Unfortunately, history repeats itself. But the current cycle is worse than the one my generation experienced. Today a terrible ritual is being enacted, through bombing, wasting human lives and all the resources of this region for military conflict, again and again. It's an immense tragedy for the Palestinian civilians of Gaza. After the entire military and political establishment was humiliated by Hamas' surprise attack, the current Israeli government thinks that the conflict can be resolved with a "rapport de force." But there will never be a permanent solution without a deep dialogue that takes into account the suffering on both sides.

These are very dark times. Nobody knows how it will end. But I believe we must maintain hope, the alternative would be nihilism, destruction, death. We must continue to try to chart a path of hope.

During the Yom Kippur War in 1973, I was part of a rescue team. For us the enemy was death: we had to save people from death. As our helicopter flew over Syrian territory, I saw villages, jeeps, and bases and that's when a missile hit us and our helicopter crashed. From rescuers we had become victims. It took me twenty-seven years to make a fiction film about this experience.

I am aware that I'm only an individual in this vast mechanism, perhaps a witness, almost in the Hitchcockian sense of the term: a witness to a crime. I wouldn't talk about mission, but there is something that I have to translate through my gaze. I recently reread an exchange of letters between Albert Einstein and Sigmund Freud on the topic of "Why war?" *Shikun* asks this question in the current context.

I often say that art may not be the most effective way to change reality, but it's a way to influence the way people think about war and conflict. And I believe that our mission as artists is to impact memory. I make films as a citizen, as a witness to the history of my country, a witness involved in what happens, as in *House* (1980, 1998, 2005), *Kippur* (2000), or *Rabin, the Last Day* (2015), about the assassination of the prime minister by a far-right Jewish student in 1995. When I made this film, it wasn't just out of admiration for a political leader—they're not people I usually admire, whether I'm in favor of or against their ideas—but out of respect for his sincerity, which is rare in politics. He could have been a general covered in victories, he was ready to go against the grain and look for solutions, and in this sense, he was both a realist and a visionary. Thirty years ago, he wanted to chart a course, to propose a valid alternative in this very complicated Middle East. And he believed that telling the truth was the basis for moving forward. This effort was decapitated by his assassination.

This raises another question: What can we do? We as writers, visual artists, painters, actors, filmmakers—is what we do totally useless? Because it's very likely that we will not be able to face such ferocious powers. Is it possible that we will lose? Yes, it's possible. Unfortunately, it is also probable. But that doesn't mean that what we do is useless, because I don't think memory is innocent. It has its own delicate way of taking its pace. In several countries around the world, we see revisionist tendencies of all kinds, who want to rewrite history in order to come to power or stay in power. But we must not allow ourselves to indulge in demagoguery and indoctrination. We must tell the truth. We need to talk about the contradictions and keep hope alive, even if we know that there are more and more destructive political leaders on the planet.

Drawing by Amos Gitai made after he was wounded during the Yom Kippur War, 1973.
Courtesy Gallery Thaddaeus Ropac

Yitzhak Rabin / Amos Gitai exhibition, Bibliothèque nationale de France, a lée Julien Cain, site François-Mitterrand, Paris, France, May 19 – November 7, 2021

Inequalities

What we don't know we don't know

Stefano Boeri

To ask what "we don't know we don't know" may seem to be a futile, even ridiculous exercise.

Yet if we only stop for a second to take our distance from the repetitive rhythms of everyday life and to reflect on what has happened in the first part of the millennium, we will realize that this question is anything but rhetorical.

In the space of just a few years, humanity has experienced four great upheavals: the attack on the Twin Towers in 2001, the financial crisis in 2008, the Covid-19 pandemic in 2020, and the war in Ukraine in 2022, followed by the tremendous situation in Gaza that is unfolding before our very eyes. Four crises, four global shocks, each of them different in its origins and effects, yet in some way interrelated.

Fundamentalist terrorism, the collapse of financial markets, pandemics, and wars between peoples are, in fact, different and extreme ways through which we might read the now unavoidable and increasingly rapid emergence of a great question regarding the future of the human species, the very meaning of our existence in the world and of our inhabitation of a small planet revolving around a star, a planet that constitutes no more than an irrelevant grain in the infinite system of galaxies.

The emerging question—to which various disciplines seek to give an answer, foremost among them anthropology, as a self-reflective branch of knowledge—is whether it is still possible to think of ourselves as a living species capable of inhabiting the world on the basis of a principle of cognitive and cultural distancing from the world itself.

Whether it is still possible to perceive ourselves as a species which is hegemonic because it is able to establish a principle of distance and otherness with respect to the rest of life on the planet. Whether it is possible

opposite page
Johnny Miller, *Inequality in Mumbai, India*, from *Unequal Scenes*, 2017

to continue to exercise the assumption of a "dualism"—between human and non-human, between culture and nature, between human technologies and natural phenomena, between the anthropic environment and natural environments—which has accompanied the development of human knowledge for many centuries.

The answer is that the four global crises of this millennium—accompanied by the continual and increasingly deafening background noise of the climate crisis—can be interpreted as dramatic invitations to go beyond the founding dualism (or rather dualisms) of centuries of evolution of human knowledge.

We have understood, in fact, that fundamentalist terrorism cannot be treated as a distinct issue that can be circumscribed to geographically defined territories and cultures, but is rather a phenomenon generated in the thick of the globalization of human cultures.

Just as we have understood, to our cost, that great financial crises—beginning with the crisis of subprime mortgages—are inextricably linked to our social expectations and ambitions.

On the other hand, nothing more powerful than the pandemic of Covid-19, a microorganism that multiplies in the bodies of individual members of the human species, could bring us abruptly face to face with the fragility of our clumsy attempts to think of ourselves as "different" from nature and from its (vegetable and animal) manifestations that we have tried so hard to keep outside our bodies, our houses, and our cities, built over the centuries as exclusively mineral environments.

Finally, how can we fail to understand that the flare-up of wars of aggression, of genocides for the conquest or rule of territories, is the crudest demonstration of our belonging in toto to the animal world and to its cruel dynamics of competition for survival.

The truth is that the erosion of dualisms, particularly the dualism between human and non-human that constitutes the conceptual premise of our being in the world, has had and is having an immediate role in the extension of the sphere of the unknown, of what we do not know, do not map, and do not control.

It is a radical development that has the tone and the potency of a new perspective on the world.

For while it is true that for centuries we have measured the evolution of our species on the basis of a criterion of progressive extension, of gradual mapping of areas of the world still unknown, this perspective now seems to have become fragile, uncertain, and insufficient.

It is certainly true that the natural sciences and the human sciences have accustomed us to measuring—with varying degrees of precision—that which we still do not know: about the universe (95% still not visible), the ocean (95% still not mapped), the lands above sea level (of which we have anthropized barely 5%), even of cerebral synapses.

However, the point is no longer simply to extend this 5% and thus to widen our knowledge in order to gradually fill these vast gnoseological gaps.

The point is that, in the age of the end of dualisms, of the mixture between living beings, of the interpenetration of cultures, of the collapse of our ambition to recognize the final limits and horizons of the phenomena of the world we inhabit, we still do not have even a vague idea of what 100% is, of the total and effective field still to be explored.

The forests, the fauna of the ocean, the depths of the galaxies, the neuronal connections, and the changing dynamics of migratory fluxes no longer seem to us to be measurable in their maximum vital and geographical extension. This is not only because we have understood that their multidimensional nature cannot be pinned down to a quantitative measurement, that is, to a horizon in relation to which we can evaluate the growth of our knowledge "geographically," but above all because our life, our aspirations, and the trajectories of our thought inhabit the multidimensional nature of these phenomena.

We ourselves are included within this non-measurable totality.

We should probably abandon the ambition to gradually conquer the territory of the unknown, as if it were a battlefield, but rather explore it with the attitude of the *flâneur* who, aware of the miscellany of the beings and the entities that flow through the world and therefore through us, chooses the challenge of empathy: the ability—in this case, a totally and exclusively human ability—to see with the eyes of other species and other living beings, and to map the confines of the contemporary unknown from these varied perspectives.

The irony of this befits those who know full well that there is nothing more anthropocentric than aspiring to conquer and represent the point of view on the world of those who inhabit it with us in an entirely arbitrary way.
What we don't know we don't know is not, therefore, the realization of a limit, but the perception of a form of knowledge that respects the unknown, sometimes embracing it, sometimes crossing it, sometimes dodging it. But always accepting it as a constant presence of life.
The truth is that the brief period in human history in which we were under the illusion that a powerful technological innovation—the boom of the digital sphere and immaterial forms of communication—could reduce and even erase not only geographical distances, but also social differences and race and gender inequalities, is now behind us.
The rhetoric about a globalized world has been swept away by the already mentioned four major crises that have affected and at the same time differentiated the geography of the last twenty years: fundamentalist terrorism, with the rigid contrast it entails between different faiths and regions in the world; the subprime crisis of 2007/2008 and the social chasms created by financial speculation; the Covid-19 pandemic, with the emergence of generational fragility alongside economic and social vulnerability; and, finally, the wars in Ukraine and in Gaza with their violent geopolitical contrasts between dying empires, established empires, and rising empires.
With the gradual evaporation of the very concept of globalization, the issue of inequality has powerfully returned to the center of contemporary history. One important reason for this is that it is fueled by the three major energies—global energies, in a way—which are redefining the differences in the biospheres of our planet:
- global warming and the vast climate migrations resulting from it;
- artificial intelligence and the immense transformations in the organization of labor;
- the rejection of biological determinism in (institutional) codes of gender identification and the emergence of plural forms of expression in the lives of millions of individuals.
After all, the loss of effectiveness of any rigid binary organization (city-coun-

try, wealth-poverty, center-periphery, public-private, material-immaterial, believer-non-believer, male-female, health-disease) only confirms that the issue of growing inequalities in the present condition of humanity calls for a plurality of perspectives and interpretive keys.

The contemporary world, its cities, suburbs, informal settlements, large urbanized country areas, and agricultural and mountain hamlets: all the living and working spaces of the human species are traversed today by multiple and sometimes contradictory drives, which tend to exacerbate racial, social, religious, and cultural differences.

These include the fundamental difference related to individual social mobility dynamics. Undoubtedly, in contrast to the growing phenomenon of the migration of bodies between distant areas of the planet, what is being curbed today in cities worldwide is primarily the social mobility of individuals—that is to say, their ability and opportunity to acquire a different educational qualification, change social status, improve their economic and cultural condition, and make transitions across the spectrum of gender identities over the course of their lives.

We should map inequalities while at the same time searching for the most advanced political projects to build a society in which differences constitute an intentional and mobile value and resource, to be recomposed within new forms of community.

This research is intended to highlight not only the sphere of urban communities, but also the biopolitical sphere of individual bodies.

We are now beginning to understand how closely intertwined the two primary challenges humanity will face in the coming years are: a necessary ecological transition for the survival of our species on planet Earth, and a strenuous campaign to reduce the growing income, gender, geographical, and social inequalities that have created enormous rifts in human societies in recent decades.

The powerful emergence of the "Loss and Damage" issues by Global South countries at the last COP in Sharm El-Sheikh—countries responsible for a very limited share of annual CO_2 emissions but the main victims of the effects of global warming and its dramatic consequences on the climate—has forcefully introduced a new perspective on ecological transition poli-

cies and, more broadly, on the overarching theme of sustainability. The truth is that today it is no longer possible to promote a policy of environmental improvement, reducing the damages of climate change and its effects on daily life, without considering to what extent such policies and actions contribute to exacerbating or reducing existing inequalities in human society. Or, more precisely, in the cities of human beings. Because it is precisely in cities that the two challenges of reducing global warming and overcoming inequalities intersect. Cities are where the challenge of the coming decades will be won or lost.

The world's cities alone, which currently occupy only 3% of the Earth's surface, produce 75% of the carbon dioxide that, accumulating in the atmosphere, generates global warming and its disastrous effects on the planet's climate. This is an increasingly critical factor as cities around the world will continue to grow in the coming years, fueled by large migratory flows resulting from the abandonment of rural areas and the flight from desertification-prone areas. Tens of millions of women, children, and families are forced each year to leave their countries and rural areas affected by desertification and drought to reach major cities in the northern part of the world, at the risk of their own lives.

As we know, it is projected that by 2050 there will be over 200 million climate refugees and migrants (source: Oxfam, 2023). Therefore, cities, where more than 60% of humanity now resides, where the maximum carbon dioxide is produced, and where the greatest efforts are being made to reduce the consequences of global warming, are the site of the next and decisive challenge for the future of humanity. Without the leadership of cities, without their coordinated and shared action, there is no hope that the states and nations of the world can achieve the climate goals proposed in 2015 by COP21 in Paris.

If cities cannot address the major challenge of reducing and containing income, social class, and education inequalities, if they cannot reduce disparities in access to services, information, and data, any policy for ecological transition is doomed to fail.

These are access-related inequalities: access to places, goods, and technologies that promise to reduce the effects of global warming on our lives and

that often, too often, are still a privilege. But also access to culture, knowledge, and education—which alone allows a path of social and economic growth. Too often, policies for ecological transition focus on designing privileged places. Privileged because they are immersed in greenery, shaded, devoid of fiery expanses of surface parking lots, equipped with all the services necessary for the daily lives of citizens that can be reached on foot, by bicycle, or with convenient public transportation.

Because they ensure that those who inhabit them have control over information and data. The truth is that too often these privileges are not accessible to the vast majority of the citizens of our cities.

Without fairer, more egalitarian cities capable of distributing the benefits of cleaner air, abundant drinking water, and a balanced diet to all citizens and not just to small minorities; without fairer cities capable of offering public spaces and shaded areas, affordable schools, and ensuring effective social mobility based on purely meritocratic criteria; without cities that are smarter and fairer not because they are equipped with digital control devices, but because these devices are accessible to all citizens at all times; without fairer cities, where the gap between central areas inhabited by the wealthiest and the marginalized outskirts where the majority of the poor live is reduced; without all this, no real ecological transition will ever be possible. Without cities willing to address the huge and growing economic, cultural, and housing imbalances between increasingly wealthy minorities and the majority of increasingly poor citizens, any claim of climate improvement will be in vain.

And we will inevitably be destined to lose the great challenge of the survival of the human species on our planet.

Index of Names

Index of Places

Index of Artworks

Photo Credits & Copyrights

- Photo © Claudia Beretta/ Archivio Claudia Beretta/ Mondadori Portfolio
  p. 2
- Photo © Laura Stevens
  pp. 3, 255
- © Agav Films
  pp. 60, 64, 74, 84–85, 96, 101, 104, 154, 165, 184, 194–95, 242
- © Christian Berger
  pp. 70–71
- Agav Films © Bernard Hébert
  p. 79
- Rita Guglielmi/Alamy Stock Photo
  pp. 86, 94, 95 center
- Stefano Boeri's private collection
  p. 91
- Photo © Abbrescia & Santinelli
  p. 95 right
- © Amos Gitai
  pp. 109, 193, 254
- © All rights reserved
  pp. 111, 222
- Multiplicity: Stefano Boeri, Maddalena Bregani, Francisca Insulza, Francesco Jodice, Giovanni La Varra, John Palmesino, Maki Gherzi, Paolo Vari
  pp. 112, 114 top
- © *La Repubblica* for the reportage "Naufragio Nave Fantasma 1996," 2001, edited by Giovanni Maria Bellu
  p. 114 bottom
- Frame from the short film *Troiane*, produced by The Blink Fish for Stefano Boeri Architetti. Director: Stefano Santamato, Producer: Paolo Soravia
  pp. 118–19, 120, 124–25
- Photo © Paolo Rosselli
  pp. 127, 144, 151, 171, 238–39
- Photo © Avshalom Sassoni
  p. 130
- Multiplicity: Stefano Boeri, Maddalena Bregani, Marco Gentile, Maki Gherzi, Matteo Ghidoni, Sandi Hilal, Isabella Inti, Anniina Koivu, Alessandro Petti, Salvatore Porcaro, Cecilia Pirovano, Francesca Recchia, Eduardo Staszowski, Kasia Teodorczuk
  p. 138

- Multiplicity: Stefano Boeri, Maddalena Bregani, Maki Gherzi, Matteo Ghidoni, Sandi Hilal, Alessandro Petti, Salvatore Porcaro, Anniina Koivu, Francesca Recchia, Eduardo Staszowsky

p. 139

- Multiplicity: Stefano Boeri, Maddalena Bregani, Maki Gherzi, Matteo Ghidoni, Sandi Hilal, Alessandro Petti, Salvatore Porcaro, Anniina Koivu, Francesca Recchia, Eduardo Staszowsky. Field work and video shooting by Sandi Hilal, Alessandro Petti and Salvatore Porcaro

pp. 140, 141, 142, 143

- Photo © Giovanni Nardi

p. 148

- *São Paulo Calling*, curated by Stefano Boeri and Lorenza Baroncelli. Promoted by Secretaria Municipal de Habitação – SEHAB, Ricardo Pereira Leite (Secretário Municipal de Habitação). Scientific Committee Coordination: Elisabete França, Lorenza Baroncelli, Eliene Rodrigues Coelho, Maddalena Bregani. Scientific Committee: Antonio Ottomanelli, Azzurra Muzzonigro, Carlos Marios Rodriguez, Francesco Careri, Francisca Insulza, Gaetano Berni, Giancarlo Mazzanti, Matias Echanove, Michele Brunello, Pietro Pezzani, Rahul Srivastava, Silvia Orazi

p. 153

- Photo © Dan Bronfeld

pp. 166–67

- Photo © Iwan Baan

p. 168

- © Domenico Gnoli, by SIAE 2024

p. 174

- Photo © Riccardo Bianchini

p. 175

- Image © Stefano Boeri Architetti

pp. 176, 183, 217, 218 bottom

- Image © The Big Picture

pp. 182, 213

- Photo © Pieter Hugo

p. 196

- Artwork by J. L. Castelli. Print by Lichtert & Fils, Bruxelles

p. 200

- Image © Stefano Boeri Interiors

p. 203

- Artefact/Alamy Stock Photo
  pp. 204–5
- Agav Films © Dan Bronfeld
  p. 206
- Munio Gitai Weinraub Foundation
  pp. 209, 210, 211, 231 top
- Photo © Dimitar Harizanov
  p. 218 top
- Developed by Consorzio LaMMA. The model offers a resolution of approximately 10 km for the Mediterranean basin, and wind data are provided by the BOLAM model initialized with GFS data at a 25 km resolution
  p. 221
- Photo © Gabriele Basilico
  p. 231 bottom
- Photo © Vincenzo Cottinelli
  p. 232
- Photo Ugo Mulas © Ugo Mulas Heirs. All rights reserved
  p. 241
- Agav Films © Laurent Truchot
  pp. 248–49
- Photo © Johnny Miller
  p. 256

The Publisher may be contacted by entitled parties for any iconographic sources that have not been identified.

The dialogues titled "Building Futures," "The Resurgence of Fireflies," and "The Memory of a House" were previously published in:

Building Futures: "Amos Gitai e Adrian Paci, una conversazione moderata da Stefano Boeri," meeting at Triennale Milano during the Milano Arch Week. Published in Leonardo Caffo, Azzurra Muzzonigro, *Costruire futuri. Migrazioni, città, immaginazioni* (Milan: Bompiani, 2018).

The Resurgence of Fireflies: "Torneranno le lucciole," *Robinson – La Repubblica*, May 16, 2020.

The Memory of a House: "La memoria di una casa," *La Repubblica*, May 9, 2023.

The Glossary texts titled "Solid Sea," "Unheimliche," "Vertical Forest," "Vivre Ensemble," "Others," and "Renato" were first published in *Urbania* (Rome: Laterza, 2021).

The Glossary text titled "Perception," was first published in *Cose spiegate bene. La Terra è rotonda*, edited by Il Post, Nicola Sofri (Milan: Iperborea, 2023).

For this publication, the abovementioned dialogues and texts have been extensively edited and revised, resulting in versions that may differ significantly from their original forms.

Authors
Stefano Boeri
Amos Gitai

Editorial team
Alberto Berruto
Maria Lucrezia De Marco
for Stefano Boeri

Marie-José Sanselme
for Amos Gitai

Acknowledgments
Special thanks to:
Giovanni Agosti
Archivio Ugo Mulas
Gabriele Basilico
Emma Boeri
Maddalena Bregani
Silvia Brena
Colline Faure-Poirée
Maura Genovesi
Michael Gordon
Rachel Henig
Richard Ingersoll
Guoyin Jiang
Patrick Jeanneret
Rivka Markovitsky
Maurizio Molinari
Mara Pannella
Thaddaeus Ropac
Stefano Santamato
Laurent Truchot

Art Direction and Graphic Design
Cristina Menotti

Translations by
TperTradurre S.r.l.
(French to English and Italian to English)

Published for

MONDADORI
ELECTA

by Mondadori Libri S.p.A.

ISBN 978-88-918-4072-1

First edition: October 2024

This volume was printed at D'Auria Printing
Printed in Italy

PEFC
PEFC/18-31-954
Certificato PEFC
Questo prodotto è realizzato con materia prima da foreste gestite in maniera sostenibile e da fonti controllate
www.pefc.it